THE DREAM ALCHEMIST

A WOMAN'S SEARCH FOR LOVE, BLISS, AND FREEDOM ACROSS INDIA, TIME, AND DREAMS

A MEMOIR

ANNA-KARIN BJORKLUND

ARS METAPHYSICA

an imprint of Sunbury Press, Inc.
Mechanicsburg, PA USA

ARS METAPHYSICA

an imprint of Sunbury Press, Inc.
Mechanicsburg, PA USA

For information about special discounts for bulk purchases, please contact Sunbury Press Orders Dept. at (855) 338-8359 or orders@sunburypress.com.

To request one of our authors for speaking engagements or book signings, please contact Sunbury Press Publicity Dept. at publicity@sunburypress.com.

ISBN: 978-1-62006-035-3 (Trade paperback)
ISBN: 978-1-62006-044-5 (Mobipocket)

Library of Congress Control Number: 2017960450

FIRST ARS METAPHYSICA EDITION: November 2017

Product of the United States of America
0 1 1 2 3 5 8 13 21 34 55

Set in Bookman Old Style
Designed by Crystal Devine
Cover by Lawrence Knorr
Edited by Erika Hodges

Continue the Enlightenment!

For all beautiful souls somewhere in time,
and my beloved daughter, Angelina

CONTENTS

PREFACE

"Transform yourselves into living philosopher's stones."
—Gerhard Dorn[1]

IF YOU ONE day find yourself inside the sacred walls of a small ashram in Southern India, where the chattering monkeys living on the grounds will try to grab your fruit if you sneak a banana or an apple out of the cafeteria after lunch, there is a good chance you're amongst other spiritual devotees who have come to live a more awakened life, reach a higher consciousness, and connect with their higher selves on a powerful inner journey.

Traveling to India to explore spiritual teachings, practice yoga, and retreat into blissful silence has become a widespread practice among seekers from all over the world, and is no longer just an experience reserved for the rich and famous, or advanced yogis. It's an inner adventure that attracts people from all walks of life who have decided to answer their inner calling and live life in higher consciousness.

Flowing into our lives like a magnificent river, the inner calling to evolve produces ripples and currents that swirl through every area of our lives, ultimately leading us on a journey of awakening. Answering the call of our soul and embarking on a soul journey seldom comes without trials and ordeals however. When we begin to truly see ourselves the way we are, including our longstanding emotional patterns, the trip is not always a breezy jaunt in a canoe. The path of inner transformation is often accompanied by elements of despair no matter how we pursue it. But the alternative, ignoring our calling and continuing to live in a foggy daze, is where the real danger lies.

Waking up to a higher awareness and learning to lovingly honor our souls becomes inevitable after we receive an invitation to grow. Once drawn into a transformational process, many spiritual seekers choose to receive divine guidance and inspiration from a guru, an enlightened spiritual guide. The omnipresent bond that is formed between a guru and a seeker, who is known in ashrams and spiritual communities as a devotee, can accelerate the awakening process and make it easier, brighter, and lighter. For some devotees, the relationship can also bring on confusion and anguish. This kind of internal disorientation is something I got to experience firsthand after returning home from India.

Awakening is a beautiful journey of soul growth which ultimately brings about higher awareness, and above all, a loving acceptance of ourselves. This book is a memoir of my own adventure at a small ashram in India, and the philosophical remnants that followed – a golden process of soul growth, the majestic journey of stepping into my own power, and finding the path of self-love.

I believe the journey of our souls is the alchemical work we do on our inner states, and I think we are all alchemists-in-training with great potential. The radiant gold we are seeking lies within. With the right attitude, we all have the power to create a loving life.

Everyone's spiritual journey is unique. Our interpretations of experiences with specific gurus, spiritual schools, ashrams, and various systems of thought differ. There are many amazing places around the world we can go for soul-enriching experiences, and I do not wish to point spiritual seekers in any particular direction. Being in the presence of enlightened and masterful beings, gurus and other kinds of lightworkers can wonderfully support our spiritual awakening. For me personally, I've found that the most sacred path of them all is loving and honoring myself, and living in a state of gratitude. Even though traveling to a faraway land is, of course, exciting, there is no need to go anywhere for awakening.

All the answers are inside us.

Anna-Karin Bjorklund

DISCLAIMER

THE STORIES PORTRAYED in this book reflect re-collections of events drawn from my own life. Names, locations, and identifying characteristics of certain people in the book have been changed to protect their privacy. Dialogue has been re-created from memory, and may not always portray what actually happened. Likewise, I have inserted universal spiritual discussions points as "teachings of the dasas." In no way do these represent a particular religion, guru, or spiritual organization, but are solely used to add context to the spiritual process of being at an ashram. To honor the privacy of my guru, I have chosen not to reveal their name or the name of the ashram. In this memoir, my guru is called Sri Brahman, which in Sanskrit means the "ultimate reality."

PART I

1.

A BLISSFUL JOURNEY

AH, I'M FINALLY here! Heathrow Airport. I walk swiftly down the corridor of Terminal One and excitedly take in the familiar ambience of travelers rushing about in every direction. I still can't quite grasp that I'm really doing this. After all the travels I've been on, I'm finally going on a true soul journey, just for me. I'm going to India.

I take a deep breath as I pass by the Longchamp travel bag shop and enjoy the aroma of fresh coffee from the Starbucks next door. *Mmm. Coffee.* I'm tempted to have a cup, but I'm not going to. Ever since I committed to making this journey I've been avoiding anything I deem unhealthy. I'm doing pretty good with it. I haven't had coffee, or any other caffeinated beverages for that matter, in over two months.

As I walk down the airport corridors, there's a rush of energy pulsing through my body. This is what I do. I'm a traveler at heart. You could even call me a globetrotter. New countries, cultures, experiences, and people have always supercharged me, which could explain why I have spent most of my adulthood moving from place to place, living in over five countries on three continents. My passport is stamped with far too many corporate trips to call me a true adventurer, but I sure travel a lot, and I love every minute of it.

With a spring in my step, I enter the British Airways lounge, where an alluring breakfast table greets me bursting with fresh croissants, colorful fruits, coffee, juice, and cheese. I munch on a handful of grapes and pour myself a glass of freshly squeezed grapefruit juice.

I've always had a secret admiration for airports and hotels. It's all the anticipation in the air I think, of travelers mingling about, on their way somewhere, anywhere. Travel is a bit of a bug for me, but a good one, at least as far as I'm concerned. My desire to travel and explore new places has been a blessing, filling me with unique experiences from many incredible and exotic places of the world. From the African savannah and the Australian Outback, to tropical islands and big cities, I have visited diverse environments and met incredible people. I've treasured my global travels. Underlying the fun and glory, however, has been a continuous search for something inexplicable. On this trip, I'm hoping—finally—to find what I've been seeking: an inner sense of peace.

I've worked in the aviation industry for many years, jetsetting around the world, generally traveling further and seeing more places in a month than most people do in their whole lifetimes. As if it wasn't enough to travel for business, whenever I have a free weekend or some time to spare, I often jump on a plane and head somewhere. I go anywhere I can, sometimes making the trip all the way back to Europe from California for just a couple of days. It's like I have to go somewhere. All the time. Anywhere.

The truth is that I've finally reached a point where I'm longing for more serenity in my life. That's why I am going on this trip. I want to feel peaceful and free wherever I am in the world. The plane I'll be boarding in just a few minutes is taking me to a small spiritual place in Southern India where I already know the energy is divine all around.

I felt this energy a couple of months ago, during a satsang (Sanskrit for a spiritual gathering), led by a woman who had just come back from the same place. At the satsang, I had one of the most profound inner experiences of my life. I floated out in a golden divine field, and all I could feel was light and love.

2.

THE CALLING

IT WAS A cold and rainy November evening. I was nestled at home in my cute little oceanside cottage in Laguna Beach, California, when I received a phone call from my aunt. She told me how she had been to a remarkable meditation event in San Diego the day before "led by a Norwegian woman with great energy," and how the same woman, whom I shall call V, would be in Anaheim that evening at a venue only a thirty-minute drive from where I live.

I looked at my watch. The event was starting in half an hour. I could still make it if I left that minute.

I had only just returned from New York and felt tired. On top of that, it was pouring rain. Driving from Laguna Beach to Anaheim in a downpour was not appealing to me, but I knew I had to go. I felt it. I jumped in my car and headed straight there. I got to the event late, but as luck would have it, found an open seat in the middle of the room. A beautiful woman was sitting on the stage all dressed in white, and her joyous eyes were absolutely radiating good energy. With wavy long blonde hair flowing all around her, she truly looked like an angel. She chanted some Indian mantra, and it sounded so amazing. I closed my eyes and enjoyed the serenity it gave me. Suddenly I felt two hands on top of my head. I opened my eyes to see who it was, but to my surprise there was no one there. There were a few people walking around with their hands gently in prayer, but there was not anyone anywhere near me. *How bizarre,* I thought. I closed my eyes again and resumed my meditation. When it happened again, I decided to just let it go.

What followed after that felt truly miraculous. My consciousness started floating out in all directions, as if I was no longer contained inside my body. I'd heard about this type of experience, but had never previously experienced it myself. It was just golden air around me, and I was floating in it. I felt home.

After the meditation ended, I went up to the stage to thank the woman for this radiant and blissful evening, and she told me she'd recently been to India where she had visited an ashram led by a wonderful guru, named Sri Brahman. As she spoke his name, she gracefully turned toward a picture on a little round table next to her that showed a charismatic-looking, elderly Indian gentleman with sparkly eyes smiling broadly at the camera. She explained that the sensation I'd experienced that evening was a pure connection with divine energy.

She must truly have reached a miraculous frequency, I thought, *because she positively radiates love. My goodness, she looks like a goddess!* To be honest, I wasn't as interested in hearing nearly as much about her guru as I was in learning more about this amazing connection I had just experienced. She told me she has been initiated by Sri Brahman to share this divine frequency, and now travels around the world to help people reach higher states of consciousness.

I was mesmerized that night. I'd never before experienced anything quite like this. Who would have known? It turned out that listening to ancient Sanskrit chants, reaching a sacred connection, and being in the presence of a divine channeler was just what my soul desired. *I want to go to India. I want to help people connect with divine energies just like she does,* my whole heart was singing to me joyfully. *This is it!* I want to be a channel of divine love and light.

That was the evening I heard the calling. I just knew I wanted to experience more of this divine energy – to make this beautiful connection a permanent state. Soon afterward I booked my ticket and was on my way to deepest India.

Did I really need to go to India to connect with this beautiful energy within me? Probably not. But I was so excited, and since

I had always loved being surrounded by spiritually minded people, I rhetorically asked myself: *What better place to go than to a real ashram in India, where I can fully devote myself to sacred connection? After all, India holds some of the richest spiritual traditions in the world. This place has got to be miraculous if it always feels like this.* The energy that night was clearly coming from a divine frequency, and I felt it. Everywhere.

3.

DEVOTED PREPARATION

My trip to India begins on New Year's Day of all days—and what better way to ring in the New Year. Even though I spent last night hanging out with friends in London, I am feeling very good and refreshed. I've been living such a healthy lifestyle lately that I even stayed away from champagne at midnight.

Luckily, the town I live in is not only one of the most picturesque towns I've ever seen, but everyone is also really nutritionally conscious, so it hasn't been that hard to keep a healthy commitment. Not only have I steered clear of coffee, I also haven't had any alcohol, meat, or dairy for a couple of months now. It is a win-win; it's doing wonders not only for my spiritual consciousness, but for my figure as well.

I have been self-conscious about my weight since putting on fifteen pounds in just one year when I worked as a tour guide in Cyprus in my early twenties. I eventually lost the extra pounds, but it was a true struggle, and ever since then it's been really easy for me to put on weight whenever I don't pay attention. This phase of health consciousness has been a refreshing change for me. It's an impressive show of dedication from a woman who absolutely loves café lattes and spends at least thirty minutes every day in a café somewhere. You may wonder how I resisted the lure of certain foods and beverages, but it wasn't as hard as I first thought it would be. I simply was so excited about the upcoming journey to India that I easily focused on doing what was right for my energy, and I switched to herbal tea.

I don't think I've ever been so dedicated in my life.

I have been meditating regularly every day on the beautiful Sanskrit mantra the Norwegian woman was chanting. Sometimes I put on the CD of V chanting and chant along with her voice, which drops me right back into that same field of golden energy I experienced earlier. I think all Brahman's devotees know this mantra, and I've now learned it by heart in preparation for the trip.

I don't think there are many people from Laguna Beach who have been to this particular ashram. There are only two that I know of: a lovely Italian couple who live in a hillside home with spectacular panoramic views of the ocean. I visited their home a couple of weeks earlier for a special satsang. It was a beautiful event. We all meditated to the sound of Indian music and received divine energy. Coincidentally, Tony, the husband, will be returning to the ashram for a deepening course around the same time I will now be there doing my beginner training. He has explained to me how men and women live separately and that we also will not be able to say hi to each other, as I will be practicing *mauna,* which means I'll be living in silence.

This is going to be quite an experience, I muse. I have done many interesting spiritual programs in the past, everything from daylong workshops on chakra balancing and feng shui, to weekend yoga retreats, but I never thought I would go to an actual Indian ashram one day.

Half an hour before boarding, I walk into the ladies lounge in the airport, where I refresh myself with luscious eucalyptus soap made by Molton Brown, reminding myself to get some of that soap on my way back home to the States. I look myself in the mirror and see a bright-eyed, excited, and fresh-faced woman. How I love that face on myself! I feel so full of hope and excitement. When I return my life will probably be quite different. At least I hope it will. Who knows? Maybe I'll come home a whole new woman: serene, wise, aware, and so spiritually evolved that I'll spend all my days meditating, chanting, and walking around smiling. I will meet everyone with love, and perhaps dress all in white. I might even get myself a collection of bindis to paste on my forehead every morning, so then I could be known around town as the wise girl in white who always wears sparkling Indian jewelry.

I look down at the bracelet my special friend, Richard, gave me before the trip. Richard is a man I've only recently got to know, it's still very early days, but we had a sweet goodbye a week earlier. *I'm really going to miss him.* I am just a few months out of a serious relationship, and almost all I've been doing since my breakup with Michael has been to focus on my spiritual development. I feel so blessed to have met Richard. He is very spiritually evolved. It puts a smile on my face just thinking about him.

I make my way over to the gate where my plane would shortly depart and think about how the people in my life have reacted when I've told them I am going to India. Some, like my aunt, have seemed genuinely happy for me, and I can really feel how they are yearning with all their hearts and souls to take off on a similar soul journey themselves, whereas others have weird expressions on their faces. They look uncomfortable, as if they don't know what to say in response to my news. I guess the idea of me heading to deepest India with my luxurious lifestyle can be confusing.

The conclusion I finally have come to is this: It must look to many people like I have a happy and flourishing life because I have a successful career working with jets, earn an abundant income, and travel the world. How can they possibly know that I often feel lost, anxious, and out of place? The truth is, I know something is missing, and I am on a quest to find it.

◆◆◆

The boarding goes swiftly. I feel very comfortable inside the British Airways 747 that will take me to India. It makes sense that I feel right at home, considering that I've spent so much of my time on planes. I sit down in my elegant, oversized first-class seat purchased with frequent flyer points and look around the newly remodeled cabin. I am in the company of a lot of well-dressed business travelers, and I am pretty sure I am the only person headed to India on a soul retreat. Then I suddenly notice a woman two rows in front of me. She has a shaved head and is wearing a long, white scarf. *Hmm, maybe she's going on retreat as well?*

After liftoff, I feel drowsy. The cabin lights are dimmed and I decide I had better get some sleep so I will be well rested when I arrive. I push my seat back and stretch out my legs, feeling so thankful for being on my way.

4.

HEAVENLY WELCOME

AT ONE IN the morning we touch down at Chennai International Airport in Southern India. The terminal is buzzing with people, light, and energy. The air is very comfortable: warm, but not hot, and despite being so far south, it's actually not humid in any way. The first thing I see as I step into the baggage claim area is a sacred altar holding three statues of elephant-headed god Ganesha. The Ganesha in the middle of the altar is made out of wood and very large.

Ganesha is a highly worshipped Hindu deity, popularly known as the god of success. He is also known for removing obstacles and protecting homes from intruders and evil energy. Last year my friend David gave me an adorable little Ganesha that I still keep in my home to help watch over my house. I feel a rush of energy as I proceed to find my luggage. I have arrived at my destination.

I look around to see if I can find any clue as to where to find transportation, and to my relief I see an Indian man smiling wildly and holding a big sign reading BRAHMAN SANCTUARY, the name of my ashram. As he accompanies me to the bus his eyes twinkle happily, and with a broad Indian accent he says, "Brahman Sanctuary is not like heaven . . . it *is* heaven!"

I laugh, and feel so happy. He might be right. I am going to a sacred place, where everything is connected. There is nothing bad there, just goodness. I am going to heaven on earth. I smile at the bus driver with all my heart, and he helps me carry my bag to the bus.

For once in my life, I'm traveling light. I stopped by the company's European office while in London and left heaps of winter clothes behind, along with my computer. What would I need a computer for on the Indian countryside? It feels wonderfully relaxing to travel with so little baggage. It makes me think of a time when I was living in Sydney, Australia many years earlier and my mom came to visit. I was in my early twenties. We embarked on a grand adventure together, flying up the coast, staying in the rainforest, snorkeling in the Great Barrier Reef, and then heading back to the city on the overnight train. Up in Cape Tribulation, an amazing place where the jungle meets the ocean, we stayed a few nights in a little hut in the jungle. The organizers of the place had never seen travelers with such large suitcases before, let alone travelers from Sweden.

I begin laughing at the memory of us dragging around our luggage—gigantic hard plastic cases on wheels. I don't know what we were thinking! My only excuse at the time was that I was moving out of my apartment and into another upon returning to Sydney, and I didn't want to leave anything valuable in storage. We were carrying so much stuff around that we couldn't fit our bags into our rental car and we had to find a railway storage center to hold them for us.

That rainforest adventure sure taught me how to pack light! I'm very proud of my one small, neat bag right now.

As I board the bus I meet many other travelers going to the same place. The first person I see is a woman shining with joy and smiling at me. She looks intriguing. There are plenty of other seats available, but I feel drawn to her and ask if the seat next to hers is taken. She leans over and tells me excitedly how she had seen me from far outside the bus, shining as if with an inner light, and asked herself, *Who is that?*

I smile and say, "I think we're all radiating today."

The woman's name is Barbara. When I tell her where I live, she exclaims that I must know her brother, Tony. My mouth drops, as Tony is not only the only person I know who has been here before, but is now returning to this same retreat for an advanced spiritual process. The coincidence amazes me. Mere moments later, Tony himself steps onboard the bus and smiles widely as he sees me with his sister. Then the bald woman from first-class steps aboard. I can't believe I guessed right about her purpose in traveling to India. The energy is high onboard the bus, and the air is filled with anticipation. I'm glad to have two friendly companions for the bus ride.

The ride is long. First, we drive on a highway—well, a road paved with asphalt—for about forty-five minutes. Then we drive on winding dirt roads through small villages with white cows lying around like dogs for another two hours. We go deeper into the countryside, to remote rural areas. As I look out through the window, there are people wandering along the road wherever I look, many with shopping bags. It's dark out still so I wonder, *what are all these people doing up in the middle of the night?* From the window I can see open markets in all directions. Occasionally the bus stops at road crossings. Out in this rural area there are no traffic lights, and in lieu of a red light at one intersection, or perhaps serving some kind of tollbooth, I see a young boy holding down a tree branch with a white rope. As our driver beeps, the boy lifts the branch so that the bus can continue.

This would be a funny way to organize traffic in the United States, I say to myself and laugh.

It is already past four in the morning when we arrive at the ashram. I am directed to building B, which is the women's house. I slip off my shoes outside and make my way into the building through a tall double door. I look around and see a dormitory plan on the wall to the left. My name is on the list for room four, on the ground floor. This has a good sound to it, as four, coincidentally, is not only my favorite number, but also my *life number* in numerology. Life numbers signify major life events, including challenges and lessons. People with number four life paths are often challenged with situations where they need to understand the value of creating order and stability in their lives. *Coming here will be a wonderful foundation on which to build a more organized inner life from now on,* I think to myself.

As I walk into room four, which is quite large, I can't help feeling a bit shocked to see twenty beds lined up dormitory style—some even located in the middle of the room. I quickly make my way over to an empty bed in the left corner next to a window and begin unpacking some of my clothes. On the other side of the wall are the closets. Perhaps it would be more accurate to describe them as small lockers. They are the smallest closets I've ever seen. Once again I'm feeling relieved I didn't bring much stuff. In fact, my belongings mainly consist of white shirts and soft, flowing white pants. It was a good call to stop by the London office to drop off my heavy winter clothes. *Ha!* Imagine if I'd arrived here with tons of warm sweaters and was trying to cram them all into this little dollhouse closet.

Before laying my head on my pillow, I turn off my cell phone. It will be left off for the remainder of my stay; I'm not going to need it here. This is a time for going within, not for reaching out. I close my eyes and drift off to sleep knowing how special this journey is. Deep within, I know that all the other journeys that I've been on, in some way, have each helped me prepare for this special time within, the biggest journey of my life.

5.

INDECENT CLOTHING

THE BUZZING SOUNDS of morning life from the village outside the ashram grounds wake me. Even though we're in the middle of the countryside and the only way to get here is by dirt roads, there are surprisingly many people up early. The sounds are coming from a distance, but there is no doubt about it. I'm definitely in India.

There's a sweet smell of incense lingering in the air. I take a deep breath and notice having a different sensation in my chest. It feels good. I can feel my breath in a new way. Each breath is like a heavenly massage. Without planning for it, I'm breathing slowly in and out through my nose, almost like the ujjayi breathing that yogis do, but without any sound.

I walk outside. The air feels soft against my skin, and the ground is a warm shade of red. I find my shoes on the rack by the door where I left them overnight, and then follow a path that leads down to a dining hall. All the buildings here are white, and everywhere I look I see the same red soil, with a few serene-looking, well-tended patches of green lawn in between. The dining hall is large and set up like a school cafeteria with long, blue tables and plastic chairs.

I join a group of three women having breakfast at one of the tables. One of them is the woman from the plane with the shaved head. "Enjoy your last day of talking," she says.

The woman next to me leans over and whispers, "She's one of the western helpers here. You know that we can talk to the helpers, right? You can also talk to your assigned *dasa* here, even during the silent part of the retreat." In India, a guru's disciples—the teachers who disseminate the guru's message—are referred to as *dasas*. Helpers are people, often from the West, who've been initiated and are there to help the participants through the retreat.

As I'm studying the helper's bald head with curiosity, all of a sudden her face crumbles with annoyance. She's looking in the direction of a woman wearing a long skirt with high slits going up all the way her thighs. I suddenly feel self-conscious, realizing that my own outfit may not be appropriate either. I'm wearing a three-quarter-sleeved coral shirt with a yellow top underneath to cover my cleavage, which for me isn't that hard. "Do you think my top is cut too low?" I casually ask her.

"Oh yes!" she says and laughs. I detect a slight tone of arrogance in her voice as she continues with dismay, "We *are* in an ashram!"

Thoughts of shame and discomfort run through my head. *Oh dear, this is just beyond embarrassing. Who does she take me for? She probably believes I'm the type of girl who wants to show off my body at all costs and doesn't have the decency to dress appropriately at a spiritual retreat.* After finishing breakfast, I excuse myself.

On my way out of the dining hall, just as I pass a colorful fruit bowl by the door, a girl warns me not to take any fruit outside the cafeteria, especially no bananas, as the local monkeys could be vicious and dangerous when hungry and have been known to attack. Apparently a monkey had recently broken into one of the women's dormitories and was eating food and throwing things around the place, causing mayhem. That's why they now have dogs on the grounds.

I quickly walk back to the dorm along the sandy red pathway between the buildings to change into a more appropriate attire. I anxiously look around for monkeys, expecting them to flock around me, and I'm relieved to be left alone. When I get back to the room, I open up my miniature closet and replace my revealing turquoise top with a long white shirt that covers almost my entire body. That should do it.

I remember seeing a lounge when entering the building the night before, and since there's some free time before we begin, I walk over there with my blow-up thermamat to do some yoga. I do a few stretches, but then stop and quickly roll up my mat again. Yoga can wait. I want to experience more of the grounds. As I return to the room to stow my mat, I find that more Westerners have arrived. There is a lot of talking and sharing of how excited we all are. A girl from Texas tells me she has used all her life savings and put the rest on her credit card to come here. I can't help feeling worried about her. She looks poor. I even find myself feeling slightly angry that the organization couldn't have offered her a discount.

A rather large, rosy-cheeked woman with short, curly dark hair now occupies the bed next to mine. She turns to me and with joy in her eyes says, "I've just heard that registration is at 4:00 p.m."

Ah. We're finally getting a bit closer to the start. It's 11:00 a.m. and I still have a few hours to spare, so I lay on my bed and open my newly acquired book about the Mayan calendar. As I start reading it, I have a brilliant epiphany. Most scientific attempts to understand the universe are external. *Why do we search outside ourselves when we should be turning inward?* I wonder.

I am so relieved and happy to be here.

6.

SOMETHING SIMILAR IN PEOPLE

ON MY WAY to lunch, I run into two Swedish women, one's a preschool teacher, the other an architect. They tell me they are here with a big group of Swedish participants. It's funny that I would meet so many Swedish people like myself in deepest India, but then again, I'm not surprised. Most of the places I've been to around the world have been the same—even Sydney. Swedish people just love traveling and moving around the world it seems. I ask the girls if they've heard of the Norwegian woman I met in California, and they both nod enthusiastically. She regularly leads similar satsangs in Europe they tell me. It was sure lucky I got to meet her on one of her world tours, otherwise I probably wouldn't have made it here!

As I excuse myself, I see a girl from room four sitting by herself at one of the blue tables. She gives me a warm smile and nods for me to sit down. I pull out a plastic chair and sit down across from her. *My gosh, she's beautiful,* I think. I take a closer look at her. She has extraordinarily blue eyes, and long, silky brown hair. She looks at me and says with a charming broken French accent, "My name is Ananda. It's a name that was given to me fifteen years ago by a guru in Northern India, as it describes who I truly am. My original name was Chantelle.

"What does your name mean?" I ask.

"Ananda means 'perfect bliss,'" she replies.

I feel mesmerized by Ananda's whole presence, and can't help noticing the resemblance between her and my friend David. They have the same blue eyes, but there is something about her energy that reminds me of him as well. A dear soul friend of mine, David, is an artist who loves crystals more than anyone else I know. I met him in an art gallery when I was on a date with a man who'd recently become a multimillionaire. He had just sold his company for a lot of money. Instead of embracing his abundance with love and enthusiasm, however, my date seemed to have entered an existential void, and the entire day we spent together, he was walking around in some kind of daze from having taken too many sleeping pills the night before. As we strolled around picturesque Laguna Beach, we found our way into a magnificent art gallery, filled with natural wonders, gorgeous sculptures, and radiant crystals. One of the staff members approached us, and he gave us such a warm smile I couldn't help feeling joy throughout. I glanced over at my date, but he still seemed distant. I asked the attendant what his favorite piece was in whole store, and he surprised me by reaching for a small pink crystal in his pocket. "This one," he said. "Definitely this one." He placed it in my hand, and there and then I knew my life had changed. It was like electricity flowing through my body. I felt the crystal vibration. Even more surprising perhaps was my own reaction. I suddenly exclaimed, "I love crystals!" My mind was perplexed as I tasted the sound of my own words. *Really? Do I really . . .? Yes, I love crystals!*

To be honest, until that moment in time I'd never given much thought to crystals, but something changed within me in that instant. I knew I loved crystals. I wasn't just saying it. I felt it.

The man I was on a date with was probably a nice man, but I never really got to know him because of his hangover from sleeping pills, and now my focus was totally diverted to David and his crystals. I ended the date early, and as soon as I was back home, I got into my car and headed straight back to the art gallery, determined to buy myself a crystal! I ended up purchasing not only a pink tourmaline but also a green moldavite. This purchase was my first encounter with these special crystals, which soon led to a strong admiration for the entire crystal kingdom. I was fascinated as David told me how it is believed that the moldavite crystal was created about fifteen million years ago when a giant meteorite crash landed in Eastern Europe. Just as he told me how good it feels to place the crystal on your forehead, one of the assistants came up by our side, and jokingly said how they come implanted as well.

Wow. Yes. I gaze at Ananda with dreamy eyes. There are definitely similarities between her and David. The remarkable resemblance between some people has always intrigued me. It isn't only how some people look the same, but even more so how some people feel the same.

A secret life project of mine has been to one day group together people I've met around the world who I feel resemble one another somehow. I'd love to have them all stand side by side to see what really is so similar about them. Maybe they're here on similar soul missions or perhaps they vibrate on a similar frequency of energy. One thing is certain to me on this day: Resembling David or not, there's most definitely something special about this woman. It feels good just being near her.

As I walk back from lunch, one of the older Swedish ladies that I met earlier asks me and another companion from our table if she can buy us each a fresh coconut juice. I happily accept her offer. She hands ten rupees to a vendor and we all watch in amazement as he slices three coconuts open with an ax-like tool. We are served the freshly cut coconuts with a straw. There's so much juice in mine that I get the sensation that it's being refilled for every sip. I am drinking from an eternal coconut! It's truly delicious. I feel so alive and full of gratitude. All the time spent waiting today has been a wonderful way to ease into the retreat.

7.

FEMALE ATTRACTION

IF YOU'VE COME to India to practice patience, you've definitely come to the right place. The process so far has been all about waiting. I've already witnessed quite a few people expressing impatience and walking around looking upset. But I'm still smiling and feeling relaxed. It turns out that registration is not to be at 4:00 p.m. as we were originally told, but instead will be at 5:45 p.m.

I sit down on my bed for a while and make more notes in my journal. As I do, the door opens and Ananda walks in. As she strides across the room, I glance over in her direction. I can't help noticing how beautiful she looks wearing nothing but the small white towel she's wrapped in. She puts one foot up on the bed and uses the towel to dry her toned legs. Then she stands there combing her long, brown hair, looking peaceful and gazing out into space, unself-consciously naked. I look at her with fascination. She has an aura of freedom.

Many of the other women in the room are signaling their dismay at Ananda's unabashed nudity to one another, but I continue admiring her. She must have seen me, because suddenly she waves her hand, encouraging me to come over. I walk to her side of the room, feeling like I'm on my way to meet a goddess. Ananda gestures for me to sit down next to her, and I do.

She is still bare-skinned and uncovered, but it doesn't make me feel uncomfortable in any way. In fact, I'm really enjoying being near her. I'm startled to realize that what I'm feeling is infatuation. We sit there and talk for a long time. I make it back to my end of the room and laugh to myself. This has never happened to me before. I must be feeling love for everyone around me as I am experiencing everything to the maximum degree. What an amazing way to begin this retreat.

"She's quite a free spirit, isn't she?" a woman with short blond hair says to me, smiling. "Wow, fancy walking around like that, entirely naked!"

"Yes, I noticed that," I reply, smiling.

"Ha, ha," the woman says, laughing. "I would think so, since you were sitting next to her on the bed!"

We both laugh. I just feel happy. Not uncomfortable in any way. I already love being here.

◆◆◆

It's now 7:50 p.m. I'm finally in line at registration. I speak with an older lady from Texas with a hearing aid. I find out that she is a psychotherapist, now on a spiritual path, and she tells me how she has read all of Sri Brahman's books. Then she asks me if I like impressionist paintings. When I say I do, she leans in closer and says, "Did you know there is a dimension of fairies and other items that have been hidden behind the paintings?"

"Wow, no. I didn't! Do you mean, kind of like those colorful, dotted 3D pictures? I think they're called autostereograms?" I ask.

"Yes, exactly!" she exclaims.

For a long time I've been fascinated by those little dotted pictures with a 3D image hidden in them that only becomes visible once you relax your eyes so you can "see behind the picture." Likewise, I'm drawn to holograms—perhaps for a similar reason. They hold more information than initially meets the eye and teach us that at the end of the day whatever we see is all about our perception of it.

Lessons about the power of perception have been all around me throughout the day, lessons about time, beauty, social conventions, and inner peace. I am so happy the lady brought up this subject because she has helped me remember how much it excites me, and because it's analogous to the way we judge people and events.

The psychotherapist from Texas and I continue talking for a while, discussing how important it is for people to go for healing regularly, and how this should even be routine and offered as a health benefit by insurance companies and employers.

As I near the front of the line, I think to myself how enjoyable it would be to film a reality show about a spiritual development center. This is the kind of show people are yearning for all around the world.

That night I go to bed feeling so contented. The answers are inside me—I'm sure of it.

8.

ORIENTATION

I WAKE UP at 5:30 a.m. with the roosters and perhaps some of the monkeys. It's still dark outside, but luckily we have electricity in the building. The corridors are dimly lit so I only need to use my flashlight to find my route around the bed. I must be one of the first girls to wake up because there is no line for the shower yet. Actually, I'm not sure if you can even call this a shower. The apparatus consists of a tiny box on the wall with a pull string for hot water. Normally I'm a lot more particular about what I will tolerate in accommodations. I take a deep breath and smile to myself, thinking, *None of this matters.*

At 7:30 a.m., the entire community gathers outside the meditation hall. Within only a few minutes, the energy has risen to a new frequency and I feel my chest opening up. It almost feels like I'm flying, I feel so much joy inside me. Can a spiritual state really feel *this* euphoric? Is this what people are searching for when they turn to drugs?

The doors open up at 8:00 a.m. A dasa standing by the door is blessing everyone who enters one by one, sprinkling water over our heads. Her smile is so wide and her face filled with such divine love that I feel like I'm entering Paradise. One of the Western helpers places a flower-petal necklace around my neck and bows at me, holding her hands in Namaste pose in front of my heart. *Namaste* is an ancient Sanskrit greeting that means "The Divine in me greets the Divine in you."

I feel serene and spiritual as I gracefully make my way into the sweetly scented meditation hall. Indian music and beautiful chanting is filling the entire place up with wonder.

The meditation hall is divided into two sections, with women to the right and men to the left. Between the gender areas is a magnificent altar holding a picture of the ashram's founder, Sri Brahman, along with statues of Ganesha, Buddha, Jesus Christ on the cross, and a painting of Mother Mary. I sit down on the little blue foldable-cushion chair that I brought along from California and look at the altar, which is decorated with flowers in vibrant colors and celestial golden bowls.

There are a lot of dasas in this room, all young men and women. They look peaceful and radiate with bliss and joy. One of the female dasas begins by welcoming us and telling us about the importance of experiencing the sacred teachings, rather than spending our time writing down everything that is said in our journals. It is better to write down our own thoughts of what was said once we have returned to our dormitory rooms, and reflect upon the teachings in solitude. I feel relieved to hear her words, as I know I would likely have felt the urge to sit and write all day, instead of allowing myself to feel the presence of the guru and taste the teachings directly. The dasa guides us into the special mantra of Brahman. This is the same beautiful mantra that I heard V chanting on the night I experienced the feeling of inner silence and peace, and floating around in a golden energy field for the first time.

After we repeat the mantra three times together, the dasa says, "This is a very important era in human consciousness. We are in a time of change. You have already lived eons of lives, and it is now time for you to grow. The process you are here for will be like living several lifetimes, learning from all experiences." I take in her powerful words, feeling blessed and divinely guided by them. It is no coincidence I'm here. I am here for a reason.

The dasa continues, "You are in a divine place. Hundreds of people in the villages around here have received blessings and live in a very high state of consciousness, which can be felt all throughout the grounds."

Wow. This must be where the amazing feeling of having my energy field expand comes from. I could feel the peaceful sensation the minute I got here. It's like a layer of good vibrations floating through the air. Every time I close my eyes, I'm in a field of gold. It reminds me of "Fields of Gold" by Sting, one of my favorite songs. "The process you'll undergo here is a process of divine development within. This may feel like someone is always sitting by your bedside. Brahman may appear at night or you may be contacted by deceased relatives. In either case, while you are here, you'll sleep like a baby." After saying this, the dasa smiles and closes her eyes, as if to connect to a higher power. Perhaps she is with Brahman.

As I sit on my mat listening to the dasa, I take in the energy in the meditation hall and think, *how lucky am I to finally have found people like me, other seekers? All my life I've felt as if I'm the only one looking for answers and trying to understand more about life. Finally I've come to a place where I'm surrounded by loving seekers, who also feel called to grow and evolve.* The dasa looks me straight in the eyes for a few moments, then turns her gaze to include everyone in the room. With love in her voice, she says, "Congratulations on the unbelievable and extraordinary luck you've had to make it here!"

9.

MAUNA BEGINS

TODAY IS A big day. Not only is it the ceremonial beginning of the retreat, it's also the first day of mauna. For the next three weeks, we'll be spending our time in silence. A new serenity is reverberating in all directions. It's now lunchtime. As everybody heads over to the cafeteria, our feet are making red dust waves on the ground. The path to lunch from the meditation hall does not take long to walk, a few minutes at most. There's excitement in the air, but we're all walking in silence.

I can already feel the change. Even though we're walking together, we're not together. Looking at us from the outside, you would see that although we might be sharing the same path, we're really on our own sacred inner journeys.

The aroma from lunch is sweet, warm, and inviting. I love curry and vegetarian dishes, so the ashram definitely offers my kind of cuisine. As I sit down to enjoy my lunch, the dasa's cute Indian accent and amazing last words play over and over inside my head, like a musical refrain: "Your life will be effortless. Everything will flow." The truth is, I already do feel lighter.

What if I am one of the lucky souls to reach enlightenment while I'm here? I wonder. I've heard stories of people who came here and had such powerful awakenings that they laughed for days when they saw how everything truly is—how there is really nothing there. This morning we watched videos of a few previous attendees who had experienced profound moments like these, become enlightened, and were now traveling around the world giving divine blessings to people. I conclude, *my desire to come here, understand more, and reach a higher level of consciousness was definitely a calling. I have accepted my mission.*

The stillness around me is totally serene. We're not only silent, we've also been asked not to exercise. Furthermore, eye contact or communication of any sort is not recommended. The only exception to mauna should occur if we wish to speak to a dasa or ask one of the helpers about something. Contact in itself is actually not encouraged under any other circumstances, even if we see someone breaking down and crying. Emotional outbursts are powerful moments where a participant could be experiencing a breakthrough. If we were to intervene, people might never learn to get through the pain on their own, which is necessary in order to reach a higher state of consciousness.

By the time afternoon arrives, I'm beginning to feel a sense of restlessness inside me, almost like I'm wasting precious time. In order to get the most out of mauna, I need to accept the present moment fully, and explore and experience my inner world. It is precisely for this reason we've been asked not to read any books, exercise, or even listen to music. Our only approved tasks here are to write in a journal or just be. I am used to spending my free time reading or learning something, and it now feels like I've entered an empty void. I think I was born with a relentless urge to get things done and learn things. The restlessness that's building inside me seems unbearable. Imagine how much new knowledge I could have gained in just this one afternoon!

The coconut man is standing next to a little pathway outside my dormitory and I decide to head over and treat myself to a freshly cut coconut. I sip its water slowly as I take in the silence around me. I can understand the no-talking part, but why no exercise? I guess it will really allow us to better experience what's going on, rather than working it out of the body. The dasa even reminded us not to walk quickly, but to stride deliberately and peacefully.

As I walk back into building B, I take a quick look at the field between the meditation hall and the dormitory. I see people walking slowly everywhere I look. It's a very strange scene, almost as if I'm looking at a painting that moves ever so slightly.

10.

FIRE CEREMONY

IN INDIA, A sacred fire ceremony where offerings are made
is referred to as a *homa*. This ritual is held for various purposes,
such as warding off evil spirits or calling in good health. A clear
intention is set in the beginning of the ceremony. It is a sacred
occasion, and Vedic priests have practiced homas for thousands
of years. The tradition is not only popular within Hinduism, but
also Buddhism and Jainism.

This evening I had the pleasure of experiencing my first ever
homa, and now I know why it plays such a special role in so
many people's lives. We held the homa with the intention of
calling in good blessings. It was pitch black outside, and the
fire felt wonderful, spreading so much light. Three female dasas
sang and chanted for us, and dogs were walking around the fire
to protect us from the wild monkeys. We were told to offer our
blessings into the fire, and to ask to receive divine blessings,
such as having our physical, psychological, and spiritual barri-
ers removed so they would no longer stand in our way.

We prayed to god Ganesha, goddess Parvati, and god Shiva
for divine blessings, and asked for help in becoming absolutely
relaxed and knowing that we can't do anything but surrender. Maybe it was because I already had a special bond with
Ganesha, the god of success and remover of obstacles, but I

got very excited when I heard he'd be joining us tonight. Also, my Indian music collection at home happens to be filled with chants honoring Shiva, which in turn made it personal for me to be bringing his presence into the homa as well. Shiva is an all-encompassing divine energy, and he represents masculine consciousness. I had never come across Parvati before, but we were told she is the power of creation, and the feminine form of the divine. She is also Shiva's wife. What an amazing combination to bring Shiva and Parvati jointly into the homa tonight. When they come together anything can happen! As part of our prayers, we also made our thanks to Brahman.

At the end of the ritual, a dasa asked us to select a quality that we'd like to offer to the sacred fire, and explained how we'd receive this quality back many times more, maybe a thousandfold. Without hesitation, I decided to offer my awakening quality, characterized by its high vibration, enlightenment, and golden light into the fire. As I did so, I found myself transported back in time to the day when I received a Reiki attunement at the end of a crystal healing course in California just a few months earlier. The Reiki master who gave me the attunement had asked me to state a wish aloud. There was no doubt in my mind what my wish was. I wished to be enlightened. But when I had uttered these words, I noticed a flicker of surprise on her face. She was probably expecting me to wish to get married or something along those lines. She then told me how everything in my life would change during the following year. On every level.

I guess being here in India signifies a new beginning for me. So much has changed in my life already over the last few months. I am definitely on my spiritual path and still amazed that I found my way here to this remote location, of all places in the world.

Lying in bed after the homa, I felt happy and serene. My "awakening process offering" was surely going to come back to me multiplied. I just knew it would.

11.

CRYSTAL COMMUNICATION

THIS MORNING, ONE of the dasas begins the lecture session by asking the question "Who is God to me?" She talks about how truly amazing your life becomes once you have a personal relationship with God. Usually I don't use the G-word much myself. I tend to gravitate more toward phrases such as *the Universe* or *the Divine. God* has such a different meaning in the Western world, I think. It has more of a religious, than a spiritual, sound to it.

The dasa smiles knowingly, as she says, "Talk to God like you would a friend or your father and mother—all the time, not only in the morning and at night."

The sound of her voice is fading into the background, as I drift into the stream of my own thoughts. *What is my definition of God?* I know that the golden light I so often feel is divine, but I don't really see myself belonging to a particular religion. Even though I was raised a Christian, I am much more of a spiritual person, with a multifaith perspective on life. I believe that saints, deities, guides, angels, and enlightened beings are here to help us along our paths of soul growth.

I return my attention to the dasa just in time to hear her say, "In order to be connected with God, we need to have communication channels open in all dimensions: physical, psychological, and spiritual." She continues, "On a spiritual level, in order to be fully connected, we need to reach a high frequency. Whenever we reach that level of vibration, even if only for a few seconds here and there, we begin to get a glimpse of what truly is there."

Crystal therapy and chakra balancing might be ways to help people get glimpses of that state, I think to myself. *They could perhaps be the ultimate solution for making the body ready on both a physical and spiritual level for the energy of divine grace.*

After I met David that enchanting afternoon in Laguna Beach, and happily brought my first two crystals home, I soon welcomed more crystals into my life and a whole new world opened up for me. For the first time since moving to California, I began enjoying staying home on the weekends instead of hopping on an airplane. The more I studied the spiritual properties of crystals, the more I enjoyed them, and soon had a beautiful collection in my home. I also took a few crystal healing courses and then began doing healing sessions for clients, which is something I still enjoy tremendously and feel wonderful doing. In fact, I've already built quite a large client base just from doing crystal healing sessions in my spare time.

Maybe the healing work I've been doing with crystals is helping me open my communication channels. Could the Divine be inviting me to follow a new path?

12.

MEETING EVERYONE
WITH A SMILE

AFTER LUNCH WE were visited by one of Brahman's disciples, Rajeshini. When I walked in the doors, I could tell immediately that there was something different about the man sitting in front of the room. Full of charisma, he quietly radiated contentment and inner joy.

Rajeshini told us he had traveled the world twice. The first time was in the mid-1990s. He'd only recently returned from his second world voyage, ten years later. Because of the long interval that had passed between his two trips, people would often ask him if he'd noticed any difference in the societies he visited. Rajeshini happily reported, "There's an incredible difference! People have changed all around the world, and become much more open. We're moving toward global awakening."

As he sat in front of the room, his entire face shining with joy, I thought to myself, *It would be wonderful if I could be more like him: radiant, giving, and able to inspire people wherever I go.* Then I suddenly found myself transported back in time to an early Sunday morning in Sweden, sitting in a church listening to the priest as a thirteen-year-old girl in my small hometown.

Truth be told, I did not attend church much when I was growing up, so this is probably one of the few services for which

I can strongly recall exactly what was said. This particular morning, I was there as part of my confirmation series, which required me to attend a certain number of services. Little did I know that the priest was to say something that ended up having an immense impact upon my life. Standing inside the built-up podium in the altar, which in the ancient churches of Sweden looks like an open tower in a castle, the priest said, "Wouldn't it be nice if everyone met each other with big smiles on their faces! Visualize how it would be if you always had a warm smile on your face!"

At that moment, there on the church bench, I took a vow always to greet people with a smile. Not surprisingly, my nickname in school soon became Smiley, and to this day I still receive comments on a daily basis from both friends and strangers of how much I smile.

Rajeshini suddenly raised his voice and my attention snapped back into the room. He was excitedly quoting something Brahman had said one day to him when he attended one of his satsangs as a little boy: "Something incredible is happening in the world . . . the Internet! It is an outer demonstration of the connection we all have within us. Everything is connected."

I felt so inspired when I heard Rajeshini say these words. This is exactly what I've been feeling about technology, but usually whenever I tell someone how current scientific and technological developments are signs of our consciousness being raised, and being in line with spiritual evolution, they look at me with big question marks in their eyes. So many people I meet seem to think that technology is against spirituality, whereas I think of science and technology as an extension of the spiritual world, tools helping us advance consciousness. There is not a scientific world separated from a spiritual world. There is one world, and its consciousness is evolving. I bet there will come a day when cellphones will be ancient artifacts, and all that is needed to communicate across space is to connect ourselves to a common frequency.

Rajeshini was so full of wisdom, spiritual insight, and charisma, and the whole day was such a joy. He always seemed to know the answers to everything. Like for instance, when a devotee raised her hand and asked, "Why do we have a medical doctor here rather than an ayurvedic physician?" Rajeshini took a deep breath. For a moment I thought he wouldn't be able to respond, but then he smiled widely and his response was so awesome. "The reason we have a western-oriented doctor here on the grounds is that we don't have time to first find out what's wrong and then to cure illnesses during the short time you are here. A western doctor can heal acute symptoms quickly and treat injuries. Eventually, the process we do here will itself heal all causes of disease."

13.

SOUNDS OF SILENCE

LIVING IN SILENCE is peculiar. Sometimes it feels like I'm back at my grandparents' home out on the Swedish country-side. Especially today, as I hung up my clothes to dry on a line in the garden, I was reminded of how my grandmother let her linens dry out by the strawberry fields during summer. Keeping my own company opens up space for fond memories to emerge. My grandparents lived in a loving country home. They had a potato field, apple trees, berry bushes, beds of tomatoes, and a very large grass field where all the grandkids would run around. Next to their house was a picturesque lake in the midst of a lush green field where cows roamed freely. Well, it was green in the summers; in winter, it was covered in sparkly white snow. There you can definitely talk about enjoying wholesome grass-fed beef and organic milk!

My memories from my time spent in my grandparents' home fill my heart with so much love. It's interesting that I would now feel like I'm back there. Their home had a unique stillness about it. It truly was a peaceful place where you could hear birds from near and faraway. The stillness I'm experiencing right now has probably brought a personality in me to the surface that re-members how much I cherished stillness in my childhood.

Although spending my days in silence feels serene in many ways, I've also been observing a bizarre perception of subtle discord between me and the other participants. As part of mauna we do not make eye contact, so I sometimes get the sense that everyone is walking around feeling upset with one another. In the beginning, it almost felt as if people didn't like me and I was being avoided. I felt rejected. Then it dawned on me that I was probably not the only one feeling like this. We're all experiencing this strange situation together, living in sheer silence and avoiding eye contact by hanging our heads and staring down. It would be interesting to talk to someone right now to find out if anyone else feels the same way or if it's just me. Then again, I guess at the end of the day it doesn't really matter. This is a silent retreat for a reason. It's my own experience that's important to me. What other people are experiencing is their path.

It's night. I'm sitting on a small white chair in the garden in the moonlight, waiting to meet my personal dasa for the first time in about an hour. She will be my dasa for the duration of my stay here, to help guide me through our practice. I look out over the grass and think about what one of the dasas said to the entire group before our afternoon meditation. "We suffer because we feel separate."

This is a very perplexing thought! On one level, we may have created separation because we feel we need to be separate from one another to exist individually – and that is why we now suffer. On another level though, there is no need for separation, because we are all the same. I know this is true, but it's still hard for me to comprehend this phenomenon—and to truly feel we're all the same, single thing. I am connected to the grass somehow. I know that. But to what extent? It isn't that I don't feel connected to people and nature, because I do. I have dear soul friends who mean the world to me, and I feel connected to them. I also love walking outdoors, feeling close to everything. I just have a difficult time grasping that we're all the same. It naturally must be something within me that makes me feel separate, that's why I am "me." Is this wrong to feel? Do I need to reach a higher consciousness and frequency to understand this vast concept?

Suddenly my thoughts are interrupted. I hear music. Music! Not Indian chanting, but soft, acoustic guitar sounds! I look around and to my surprise I see one of the Spanish helpers sitting there, singing and strumming his guitar, looking content. *Wow, this is incredible! I'd almost forgotten how much joy music gives me.*

I look at him with curiosity. His long, dark hair is snapped back in a ponytail. He's a very good looking man. The way he's playing his guitar and singing by himself in the moonlight makes me feel all bubbly and happy inside. *Maybe music is the answer! Maybe music is what helps connect us, and bring us to higher levels, connecting us with everything and everyone.* I can't help staring at him.

He turns to me, smiles, and says, "Look at that moon!"

"Yes," I answer, then inquire curiously, "Am I allowed to talk with you, since you're a helper?"

"That's what they say," he responds in a cute Spanish accent, as he continues strumming lightly on his guitar.

I feel such a rush of exhilaration. He really is strikingly handsome. I have always felt a little weak around good guitar players, and now here at the ashram, pretty much the only man I'm allowed to talk to is sitting next to me, in the moonlight, with a guitar in his hand. This has to be fate. I smile widely at him, and I can even feel how brightly my eyes shine.

"It's best though if you can stay in your own silence," he says. "This is an important process, and you're here for a reason." He stands up, and walks back into the men's dormitory.

"Oh. Right." I clear my throat. "Of course." Then I just sit here, shocked. I can't help feeling let down, but of course I know he's right. Talking can wait, I guess. I'm here to work on something important: Myself. But still, what a letdown. I keenly feel my sense of separation.

A few minutes pass and then I walk back into the building where a lot of girls have now gathered around a notice board. I peek at it curiously. *Aha! I have a dasa!*

14.

A Case of Nerves

MY PERSONAL DASA is a tiny woman with big, beautiful eyes named Nicolita. She strode into the meditation room so peacefully this evening, wearing a long, white sari like all the other dasas. Later, we'll be seeing our own dasas individually, but tonight we have met them as a group.

It started off as a very nice evening, but I'm now lying here in my bed, trying to understand how everything could have gone so wrong. How did this beautiful day end up with me feeling so uncomfortable and nervous when introducing myself to my fellow participants, after many years of quite confidently giving corporate presentations in front of hundreds of people? I'm so disappointed in myself. I wonder what brought this on. *Could it have anything to do with the subject matter actually centering around myself this time around, rather than a business study? Why in heaven's name did I feel uncomfortable talking about me?*

We were ten women in Nicolita's group. We sat in a circle and introduced ourselves one after the other. At first I felt relieved that we were finally being allowed to talk for a while, taking a minibreak from mauna, and letting go of some built-up pressure. I treasured the initial moments of connection with the others. Unfortunately, just being on a spiritual retreat did not seem to have helped me get over the nerves I would get when I had to speak up when I was younger. Even though the group was just ten women, I sensed that old, familiar feeling of anxiety clenching me tightly around my chest. I thought I had escaped this feeling long ago.

In fact, I've been doing pretty well mastering my fear of public speaking over the last few years, learning to enjoy talking and laughing about jets and money in front of large audiences without feeling nervous at all. *Where did all the fear come from tonight, when it was time to talk about myself, someone I know well? Or maybe that's it. Maybe I don't know myself? Is that the core issue here?* I remember reading somewhere that if you don't really know the subject you're supposed to speak about, if you're not well prepared, you'll be nervous. If that is the dilemma I'm having now, it's a real blessing that I'm here to gain self-knowledge on a higher level.

My goodness! I can't live my life with a chest that feels as tight as thick rubber whenever it's my turn to take the stage and show the world who I am! I can't wait to live in a state of total flow and inner contentment. This inner anxiety has probably been keeping me from evolving. I wonder where it's coming from.

I so wish I could accept myself the way I am. I would love to find a way to love myself unconditionally and not be bothered by letdowns like the one tonight in the circle. It doesn't occur to me that the anxiety that arose within me when it was my turn to talk to the group tonight may have been partly linked to me seeking acceptance from the other members, and partly induced from feeling rejected by the guitar player in the garden. I would do anything to avoid this feeling.

15.

FAIRYTALE

THE RETREAT LASTS three weeks and we're only three days in. From now on, I'll be meeting with Nicolita about once a week, but I really hope I'll see her more often because I'm already beginning to feel lonely. Everything is so quiet. It's still early on and we've only been in mauna for a couple of days, but uneasiness is spreading inside me, weaving a pattern all over my chest like a spider's web. I've quickly learned that I'm not content spending so much time deep within myself. My thoughts feel heavy and difficult. My sense of restlessness is overwhelming, to say the least. That I am so uncomfortable with my inner world must be a sign that I've repressed a massive amount of feelings through the years, and have an underlying view of life—totally unknown to me—which I'm only just now beginning to experience. Oh. I so wish I was back in California, listening to regular music and enjoying myself with friends. That sure was a lot more fun than this! My life back home seems distant right now.

It is mid-morning with a few more hours to go before lunch, which means another long session of meditation ahead of me. As I am sitting on my cushion in the meditation hall in deep silence, my thoughts swirl around inside my head. *How did I get here?* After what feels like days, we finally break from our long meditation. The dasas are preparing to speak in front of the big room and I appreciate being taken out of myself for a bit. It was very lonesome in there this morning. Hopefully, this will be an inspiring talk.

A dasa with short, black hair begins to speak. "Most of our suffering is created by ourselves. Whatever happens to us in our lives is a reflection of what's going on inside us. If we can reach a place where we feel better inside, the outer world will instantly change. The key is to believe in receiving grace. We need to feel and believe first, before anything can happen."

It's so true. I know it is. Of course, the big question here is, even if I know that my beliefs shape my reality, am I really living as if this is so? I need to get to a place where I believe in grace and trust that I will be supported. If I could just feel that whatever I want to happen has already happened, I can attract it, but I don't know how to get to the feeling. *Clearly I need to work on myself more so I can get into the right frequency.*

With a gentle voice, the dasa continues, "To grow and heal, we need interference of grace. We can't come out on our own. We need to surrender and be helpless. This is how grace can intervene and come through for us."

I reflect upon these last words for a bit, and wonder how I can get into a helpless state and totally surrender to grace. Then I suddenly remember that I've had experiences of divine inter-vention, or grace, before—many quite recently as it happens. In fact, I was brought here with the help of grace, or should I say - a fairy.

◆◆◆

My encounter with the fairy happened just a few weeks before the satsang with the Norwegian woman in California. I was at a crucial transition in my life, a bit bored with my job, just out of a relationship with my boyfriend, and living in a new home. Whatever the reason, cause, or meaning of the fairy's visit, there is no doubt that it helped me recognize there's a lot more to the world than meets the eye.

That a spiritual shift was already underway could be seen from the way I was spending my free time. After years of contin-uous jetsetting around the world, I felt increasingly content just to stay home and read spiritual books or give healing sessions with my crystals. However, all this new time at home was making me realize how lonely I was, and I was also feeling a little sad nothing extraordinary ever happened to me. I felt unfulfilled.

I had just been to see *Conversations with God,* the beautiful movie of Neil Donald Walsh's life story. Driving home in my car, I started crying deeply. As I sobbed, I made a wish with all my heart that something truly miraculous would happen to me too someday. My whole soul was searching for something more, looking for a sign of some sort. I literally can't remember if I had ever cried so deeply before. I felt helpless, disconnected, and very sad. Little did I know that I was going to have the surprise of my life later that night.

Back home, I climbed into bed and drifted into a deep sleep. Something woke me up around two in the morning. The first thing I saw when I opened my eyelids was what looked like a butterfly sitting close to the ceiling on the window frame! I sat up in sheer surprise and looked closer. It was dark in the room, but there was enough light for me to see some details. As I squinted my eyes, a tiny, rosy-cheeked happy little girl with brown hair suddenly emerged. She was giving me the warmest and widest smile I have ever seen, filling my whole heart with divine love. She was wearing a red dress, and her wings were so sheer and precious - translucent with sparkly golden threads and fine patterns. They were shaped just like a butterfly and outstretched. A girl with wings! *An angel? Maybe a fairy!*

I was so astounded, I didn't know what to do or think. I'd never studied fairies or even been particularly fascinated by the lore about them. I thought of them as imaginary beings from fairytales. So when this little girl suddenly began flying around my bedroom, there are no words to describe how I felt. Halfway across the room her whole body stretched out before vanishing into thin air.

I was still sitting up in bed feeling astonished beyond words. Before doing anything else, I reached for my phone and sent texts about the girl first to Richard, and then to my mother.

In the morning, when I awoke, the image of the little girl was still there in my mind's eye. I kept my eyes closed and could feel something more coming to the surface. Slowly, memories from my dream world started appearing. Visions of little, brown clay houses, some leaning, some stretching up tall, were coming into my mind. I could actually remember having been there, visiting this realm. I was there. In the land of the fairies. It was so real, so vivid. I was conscious of having been in a different dimension, like I was having a lucid dream, but different, almost like an out of body experience. I could also recall a snippet of a conversation from the dream in which I was begging someone next to me not to let me forget about my time there. Perhaps the little fairy had shown up in my reality in order to remind me about my journey to her world. Or perhaps she came to my house to bring me with her on a special journey. I don't know which came first, if either.

Whether the fairy came to me before or after I embarked on my grand adventure to fairyland, and whether or not the little fairy was a dream or "real," is not really important to me. I believe many dreams involve actual journeys and visits. What matters to me is not what happens, but how we feel, learn, and grow from the experiences we have.

I reached for my phone to see if I dreamed sending the text messages. Both of the messages I remembered sending were indeed in my phone. It was exciting to have the physical proof that the fairy had really shown up—or at least that I had been awake for part of the experience.

Whatever happened that night, one thing is for sure: From that moment on, I believed in divine intervention. That night I had surrendered, and somewhere, someone was listening to my deep, heartfelt wish. A little fairy appeared and opened up my eyes to something bigger than my ordinary life. Shortly after her visit, I was introduced to Brahman's divine energy.

Look how my life has evolved, within just a few months! I mused. *Now I'm in India, deepening my spiritual growth. That must be the grace the dasa is talking about.*

16.

DIVINE RELATIONSHIP

WE HAVE JUST finished lunch and we're back in the meditation hall. One of the dasas is talking about how we can really get anything we want, but if we don't accept ourselves the way we are, believing in our own prayers can become a challenge. Before she ends her lecture, she adds, "Remember that prayer is everything. With prayer, nothing is impossible: Ask, believe, and receive." The dasa flashes us a white smile and softly closes her eyes.

I love how the dasas go in and out of meditation as they speak. It's like they are getting their words from their hearts and connect with the Divine every time they say something. Once again, what they are saying sounds like mainstream spiritual advice and so should be easy to implement. But it's not. I can't help wondering how I can get to a place inside myself where I can believe in a prayer without beginning to doubt that something I've asked for will happen. Or what if my prayers have already been answered and they're defective in some way because of inner dissonance? Maybe I haven't worked on all my inner "personalities" sufficiently, and that's why I'm having such a hard time believing what I really want. Perhaps I'm unconsciously holding on to too many negative feelings and they are sabotaging what is manifesting for me.

The dasa opens her eyes and continues, reassuringly, "You will create a different reality by inviting grace into your life and always being of service to people."

Aha. Maybe that's what I've been missing. I have not flowed with the Divine inside my heart. It is by connecting myself to divine energies that I can become a cocreator with the Universe!

Truth be told, I have not always been that helpful to others. I hope I can do more for humanity. I make a pledge: *From now on, I will enhance my relationship with the Divine in my heart, begin donating money to charities when I return home, help everyone around me, and be there for my friends more.*

As I walk back to the dormitory after meditation, I continue thinking about my personal relationship with the Divine, and what I can do to enhance it. Many devotees here have already formed a special relationship with Brahman. In the mornings before the first meditation session, people are now lining up to give their love to the guru. Lying face down on the ground, they pray with their arms stretched toward the altar. I admire them for being so openly devoted, but I can't see myself doing the same. I'm very happy to be here at the ashram, and I love the amazing energy of the community, but I'm not really the kind of girl who worships a guru—or anyone for that matter. I must admit, however, that I am sensing the presence of Brahman around me more and more. Being here in India, at his sacred ashram with the dasas talking about him so often and with so much love in their hearts, I can't help detecting a little voice inside me that wants to know, *Could I, too, be a devotee of Brahman?*

I take my yoga mat with me into the living room. I'm going to practice some light stretching. As I fold forward over my legs, I try to visualize Brahman in front of me, but I can't get a strong image of him. All of a sudden, a vision of Paramahansa Yogananda comes before my eyes. I see him very clearly, and remember how familiar he seemed the first time I saw his picture on the cover of the book *Autobiography of a Yogi*. I close my eyes and ask the Divine if I could possibly transfer my feelings about the Divine over into Yogananda, to create form and space for them, and I feel intuitively how this would be fine. I'm going to give it a try.

17.

THE ART OF SUFFERING

WALKING DOWN THE dirt road leading to the meditation building, my feet already covered in red dust, I'm sure happy I didn't bring any expensive shoes on this journey. I so hope today will be better than yesterday or the day before that. I'm ready to experience beautiful things now and see India in all its glory. The last few days have been filled with so much inner work that I'm beginning to feel really weighed down.

The moment I enter the meditation room, I'm hit by an enormous wave of sad and heavy energy. It's pretty evident that this is not going to be a day for feeling good. I choose a spot in the middle of the women's section. Once I'm on my cushion, I take a deep breath to calm my nerves. *I accept I am here, I accept I am sad, I accept I am suffering,* I repeat to myself over and over.

Just as I close my eyes, one of the dasas reminds us, "In order for suffering to go away completely, we must first fully experience it, and allow it to 'eat' us. Otherwise it will come back. When we think about how we want to move away from suffering, that is what suffering is. Suffering will come back in a different form if we don't stay with it. When we stay with the suffering it is important to pay attention to what is happening in the body. This is how we can truly experience it."

Yes. I think to myself. *Isn't this what I'm doing right now?* To accept how we feel is nothing new to me. I've heard about this spiritual practice so many times before: "If you're having a panic attack, the only way through it is to accept it, experience it, and let go. If you try to avoid it, it gets worse." These dasas are so wise and they make everything sound so easy. If I'm being honest with myself, however, it's not as easy as it sounds, because it feels uncomfortable, which is perhaps why I haven't always practiced it. Just saying the words *I accept how I feel* may not be enough for me to fully accept whatever is going on with me feeling-wise.

◆◆◆

After lunch, we are asked to meditate on our suffering. Hopefully this is exactly what I need: a deep meditation in which I concentrate on the sadness inside me. I wonder what I should feel sad about first? Over the years, I have built a wall of guilt about living abroad for so long, and for being so far away from my family in Sweden. I also feel very sad about the endings of some of my relationships. However, despite purposefully reviewing the details of my past experiences, even the sad ones, I'm not sad to the level that I want to cry like so many of the others in the hall are doing. Some of the people around me have so much pain they are crying and shouting hysterically!

I suddenly feel very confused and can't help wondering, *what's going on here? Who are these people?* It's almost becoming unreal. *Are they actors,* I wonder? *Have some attendees been hired to come here to scream and cry loudly?* I look around and I just don't know what to make of this scene. At the same time, as surreal as it is, in a bizarre kind of way I almost feel sad that I'm not as sad as some of the others. *Hmm, maybe if I think back on what went wrong in my relationships?* That should bring about some sadness.

I'm only in my thirties, but like a lot of people around the world, I've experienced a fair amount of infidelity and mistrust in my relationships. Perhaps worst of all, in my opinion, is that I stayed in them way too long hoping things would get better. First there was Gabriel, a writer who captured my heart. For the longest time, I thought he would be the love of my life. We met early one Sunday morning at a café in South Kensington when we were having coffee next to each other and both reading the Sunday paper. I was on my way for a day of polo in the English countryside, and was wearing a pretty pink dress with a red cherry pattern.

Polo, I must add though, is not one of my favorite pastimes. It is, however, the kind of sport that many Brits like to play, and at the time I loved being invited to anything that involved traditional English culture, and it also got me out of the big city every now and then. I always had a hard time relaxing at the polo matches I attended because I found the sport extremely offensive and harsh on the horses. A few times I even had to excuse myself because it was too much to bear.

I was reading a section about the new TV series, "Big Brother," in the paper when Gabriel leaned over and asked me what I thought of the show. We talked for a while and then he told me he might soon be in a similar reality show himself. We had our first date just a few days later, walking around the Serpentine Pond in Hyde Park. What followed was a whirlwind romance.

If I had trusted my gut feelings and been more observant than in love, I would have seen warning signs right away. There were often cute voicemails left by a girl called Natalie on his answering machine, and every now and then he would simply disappear as if off the face of the earth to later reappear as if nothing had happened. He would come back so full of love and tell me he wanted to get married, but then he would also carefully explain how he was not yet ready because he had no prospects of making money.

Whenever I asked Gabriel about the voicemails, he would get angry with me and say they were from a close friend of his family. Perhaps, because I've always been a pleaser, I put up with it all. I hoped the situation would get better if I just tried harder. But my suspicions were rising. One day he told me he was helping his brother with a project of some kind and I didn't believe him. I tried to get him on the phone a few times, but he never picked up.

I went over to Gabriel's house, and when I found the front door slightly open, I walked straight in. The first thing I saw was Gabriel standing in the middle of the room. It only took me a few milliseconds more to realize he had someone else with him. Seated on the sofa was a girl with long, shiny, dark hair, dressed in a red tee-shirt and shorts. I turned to her and with a racing heart and asked her, "Are you . . . Natalie?"

"Yes, I am." She was looking at me with an equally uncertain look. "Are you . . . Anna?"

"Yes, I am."

The entire room was filled with charged energy from floor to ceiling. By now Gabriel had apparently collected himself from the initial shock of having the both of us in the same room, as he suddenly shouted, "As you can see, Anna, this is not a convenient time!"

Natalie paid no attention to him, but instead looked me straight in the eyes and asked, "Have you been seeing him?"

"Oh, yes," I said, puzzled, "for the last year." Then I added, "Have you been dating him as well?"

"I thought I was," she said, twisting her ponytail.

My heart was now racing double speed, and a dizzy feeling was coming over me.

"Would you please leave?" Gabriel demanded.

With a sudden flash, the dizziness was gone and a wave of force and determination filled my entire being. "No, I think I should stay," I announced with a strong and firm voice. I sat down on the right-hand side of the sofa next to Natalie and crossed my legs. "Have you kissed him?" I asked her.

"Yes," she said, and nodded.

Gabriel's face was turning red with infuriation. There was no question about it. He was about to explode from anger.

I turned to him, "So, you haven't been to your brother's tonight? You haven't been helping him?" I felt a twinge of resentment that he had told me a lie about helping his brother move.

Natalie looked at him questioningly, and then, with a slightly shaky voice, said, "I'll go."

"Right, so shall I," I said with a flair of pretended calm and elegance.

We both rose at the same time. "Very nice to meet you, Natalie."

"You, too." She gave me a strained smile.

I got out of the apartment first, but just before I entered the elevator she caught up with me. I still couldn't believe it, I needed to hear more. "I heard your messages on the answering machine," I told her. "And he always insisted you're just a friend. More precisely, a friend of the family."

"And I've seen your text messages," she said, and sighed. "But whenever I asked him about you, he just brushed off the question, telling me you're simply a friend." She took a deep breath, and then continued, "I feel very sorry for you. Just to let you know, I haven't just been a casual fling. Gabriel and I have plans to get married. We're going to live in a house on the coast and everything."

With her face suddenly more animated, she added, "Did you call him earlier today?"

"Yes, I tried to reach him a few times. We were supposed to go on an excursion today, but he told me he couldn't go because he had to help his brother. I came over because I felt something was wrong. I told him on Friday, 'You're going to have to try harder to make this work or I won't be able to stay in this relationship anymore.'"

"That's what I said to him after Christmas!" she exclaimed.

"This is so wrong. I'm so glad I met you tonight, Natalie, because now I know why things between me and Gabriel have felt strange for so long."

I could remember walking home that night in the dark, and I wasn't really sad. I felt more relieved than anything else that finally the confusion I'd had was gone. I had been trying to understand Gabriel's behavior for so long, and the relationship was clearly not healthy for me. Still, I stayed in it for a long time and closed my eyes to all the warning signs. I just kept hoping we would find a way. We were obviously not going to, and I have finally been released from a burdensome situation that apparently had been very difficult for me to walk away from.

I looked around the meditation hall. Everybody was still freaking out as far as I could tell. *As much as I try feeling sad about this now, I'm still not crying out loud like everyone around me is. Maybe I've already processed that event enough?* I thought.

Hmm, what about Michael?

18.

HEARTBREAK

SHORTLY AFTER MOVING to California, a friend invited me to accompany her to a dinner being hosted by her ex-boy-friend. I arrived as planned, but she got caught up at work, so the party consisted of me and eight misbehaving men at a steakhouse, one behaving stranger than the other. Michael was one of them. He was the most handsome, most interesting, and least crude man at the table.

In the middle of the dinner, one guy rose from the table as if he was about to give a speech. A waitress was walking in our direction and smiled happily at us. He faced the woman with an expectant smirk on his face, and asked, "Are you up for the helicopter trick?"

I had no idea what he was talking about. Everyone else laughed, even the waitress, who put a hand on her hip, sighed, and said, "Ah, come on then. I've seen it before."

To my astonishment, the guy pulled down his zipper, took out his penis and started swinging it around in circles! I didn't think there was anything funny about this performance, and I couldn't believe it was happening in the middle of a fine estab-lishment. Our table was dead center in a fully occupied dining room. Through a miracle, none of the people at other tables seemed to have noticed, or if they did, they didn't say anything about it.

As if that wasn't all, a few minutes later another guy threw his wedding ring into my wine glass. With a big smile on his face, he asked me, "How are *you* doing?"

I couldn't wait for the dinner to end. As soon as it was time for after-dinner drinks, I excused myself and almost ran out of the restaurant. The dinner was so shocking that I wanted to forget about the whole evening. It was sheer luck that Michael and I happened to connect afterward. A few weeks later, we literally walked into one another at an outdoor summer concert. I gave him my number, and we got together the very next day.

Although we had a lot of fun together, my relationship with Michael was never a whirlwind romance, or an exclusive commitment—though I mistakenly thought it was, and it was on my part. Unfortunately, the pattern from my relationship with Gabriel began to repeat itself. Michael had not only one, but several other girls as his best buddies. They were all "special friends," such as running friends, theater friends, cooking friends, and the list of activities goes on and on. One day I dropped by his house to surprise him with a fun sweater I bought him on a trip. I had a key to the house, so when there was no answer, I happily walked in to leave it there for him. That's when I saw it. On the sofa in the living room was a neat pile of soft pink and white women's clothing.

My first thought was to get out of there as fast as I could. I turned and started heading toward the front door when it opened and Michael walked in followed by a gorgeous girl with long, black hair snapped up in a high ponytail. She first flashed me a quick white smile, and then looked uncertainly from me to Michael.

"Hi there," I said, in shock.

"Ah, Anna, what a surprise. Meet Pomena," Michael introduced his friend casually. I could feel my heart plummeting into my stomach.

"What's going on here? Are these your clothes?" I asked Pomena.

"Erh . . . yes," she replied. She then turned to Michael and said, "I'm going to jump in the shower, OK?"

I stared at her, perplexed. "Why are you taking a shower here?" I asked.

"Hey," Michael interrupted, "you're making her feel uncomfortable."

I could not believe what I was hearing. *I am making* her *feel uncomfortable?* My heart was racing at this point and my thoughts were swirling like a cyclone. I walked out the front door and Michael followed me. Outside the house, he put his hands around me and tried to reassure me of his intentions by saying that she was just a "very good friend" of his. I was too upset to talk so I went home. Later on, he convinced me I had jumped to the wrong conclusions. At the time I didn't know for sure if they were or weren't sleeping together, so I gave in. Looking back, I can see how needy I have been. I keep on pleasing people who treat me badly, in what is probably a desperate attempt to be loved. That's probably why I accepted his apology.

This was not the only time I walked out on Michael after finding him with another woman. Each time he explained it away and we would decide to "try again." This would lead to another few months of joy and happiness, followed by him bringing home more "friends," denial, and heartache. It was a never-ending story that eventually ended when he fell in love with a girl twenty years younger than him. This time he told me the truth. The girl was not just a "buddy," but the love of his life.

That was four months ago.

◆◆◆

I adjust my position. My legs are stiff.

I think the contemplation exercise is working. I am actually feeling sad about what happened with Michael, so there must still be unprocessed pain there. Looking back on my past relationships, none of them were really that healthy, but for some reason I always stayed in them and kept trying harder and harder to make them work.

I close my eyes again and images of Michael keep coming into my mind. We had moved into a loving home just earlier that year. Ah. I remember how sad I was when we first broke up. With melancholy I think of our bright kitchen, and the fun dinners we used to have.

Suddenly my thoughts are interrupted when a lady sobbing in the back of the meditation hall raises her hand and in a strangled voice asks, "What if you have lost a baby, and cried and suffered more than you thought you ever could, and you still feel sad?"

Oh my goodness. That's devastating. The dasa nods understandingly and takes a deep breath. "It is very sad, and I know how you feel," she responds lovingly. "But if you still feel sad even after truly experiencing the suffering, you have not experienced it enough."

She pauses for a few seconds, then thoughtfully adds, "When we feel hurt, worried, or upset, we need to stay with the feeling and not flee it by watching television, talking about it with a friend, reading a book, or even looking at beautiful scenery. We need to go within and experience the entire suffering process."

I wonder, *does everyone have the capacity to really suffer like that, or do some not make it?* I have always thought of reading a book or listening to music as good distractions from my pain, but what the dasa said makes perfect sense. This is, of course, why we're not supposed to read, talk, or listen to music while we're here. We need to be present with our inner lives.

I'm beginning to feel a heavy sensation in my chest and notice how very tired I am. I am so tired.

19.

INFINITY MEDITATION

I'VE BEEN SITTING here all morning with immense sadness taking over my body. The heavy sensation I began experiencing yesterday has now spread throughout my body and penetrated even deeper into my chest. It feels almost unbearable. My arms and legs are numb and heavy, and I'm very dizzy, like I have a fever.

Just as I am feeling the most sorry for myself, thinking I've lost all hope, one of the dasas suddenly announces that four elderly monks are on their way over. They're coming to give us grace and help us fully experience our suffering. There is a moment of silence, followed by the sound of the doors opening in the back of the meditation hall. In walks four elderly monks, two women and two men, dressed in long, orange capes. One of the ladies is so delicate that she needs help to walk. They move very slowly up the aisle that divides the men and women's sections, making their way to the front of the room.

I feel very touched and blessed. One by one we are invited to meet with a monk, and upon receiving grace, some people begin crying hysterically. Some break into manic laughter. When it's my turn, I am very nervous. I pray that the heaviness I've been experiencing today will go away after being blessed by these divine beings. When I come up, I see my tiny little dasa, Nicolita, leaning toward the elderly dasa who is about to offer me grace, whispering something in her ear. I feel baffled. What is she telling her? *That I don't need that much energy? That other devotees need it more?* Thoughts of jealousy and abandonment begin swirling around in my head. But as soon as the elderly dasa embraces me, I can feel love coming through her hands. She kisses me on the neck and then right on my mouth. The whole time she has her eyes closed. *I wonder if she's blind?*

Rather than linger in the dasa's embrace, I pull back after a minute, worrying that the line of people behind me needs to get their turn. I rise and walk back to my seat. I notice how many of the other participants need help returning to their seats after their blessings, but I'm fine. I lay down on my meditation mat and try to relax. It doesn't work. All the crying and screaming and laughing in the room is very disturbing, but more challenging than anything are the thoughts swirling around inside my head. *Why does my process here seem so different from that of the others? If some people are crying hysterically, and even need help walking after receiving a blessing, why is this not happening to me?*

As I lay there, again I can't help feeling sad because I'm not as sad as the rest of the group. This is just beyond peculiar.

I take a few deep breaths and then my chest becomes heavier and tighter. A shock wave of memories flows into my awareness, reminding me of all the times I've felt anxious and uncomfortable in my life. I consciously breathe deeper and deeper, filling my whole stomach with air. Then it's suddenly like my awareness level skyrockets to maximum setting. The air going down through my throat spreads out inside my chest and makes its way into areas I never even knew I could have internal sensations. My emotional pain disappears. I think, *Wow. The blessing must have activated something within me after all.* My chest feels so large, like it's been "super-sized." I lie there without moving for about an hour, maybe more, just breathing and feeling my chest expanding and resonating at a very high frequency.

I hear one of the dasas announcing over the microphone that in ten minutes we are to do a meditation in the presence of the monks and receive the blessing of their infinite energy. This is incredible. I wonder if I can take any more tonight.

At 7:00 p.m.., new monks begin slowly arriving. Well, it is perhaps not right to call them *monks*. They are divine beings with a very high level of consciousness. The dasas describe them to the assembly as "divine beings who have reached enlightenment to the maximum capacity possible while being in a human body." They are very old and all have difficulty walking and need to be led into the room, one by one. Apparently they meditate most of their existence now, they hardly need any food, and just being in their presence raises one's awareness.

The infinity meditation the monks do with us turns into one of the most beautiful experiences I've ever had. I pray for higher consciousness, inner calm, enlightenment, and that my gift will be to share it with as many people as I possibly can.

20.

THE DIVINE TAKES FORM

WE'VE JUST FINISHED morning meditation. I'm sitting here determinedly, with my legs crossed and my hands casually resting on my knees. Today I've decided to give suffering a real go. After all, I am here to evolve and reach a higher consciousness, and if this is what we need to do along the way, I'm going to show up and do my part. I've always been a conscientious and dedicated student, and what could be more important than working on myself and growing?

It's pretty easy to suffer now. In fact, I'm impressed with how good I am at making myself suffer in just a flash. All it took was simply imagining how much I would suffer should Michael and I ever get back together again. Possible scenarios with new girls kept flowing into my mind like waves crashing on the shore. Isn't it funny? None of those new imaginary situations has even happened, but just thinking of how they might has my entire chest clenching. I remind myself to keep experiencing the pain and continue to breathe deeply. Slowly my chest fills with air, and voila, it happens- the pain eases!

Now I know how to reduce anxiety when it flows in: The trick is first to feel what's happening, and then to continue breathing in until the whole chest is filled with air. I know this is not the ultimate solution for my anxiety though. The real dilemma I'm tackling, and need to face up to in myself, is finding out why the anxiety occurs in the first place. Tools are wonderful to have, but I would love to get to a point when I don't even need to use them, and never have to cure myself from feeling anxious.

I remember one of the dasas telling us how everything wants to survive, including fear. The anxiety within me must be fighting hard to survive right now.

◆◆◆

Before our afternoon meditation session, we have individual meetings with our personal dasas. As I sit down beside Nicolita, I feel very connected with her. She is so present. I tell her about my struggles to translate my notion of the Divine into a form, and that I am actually trying to use the image of Yogananda right now.

She smiles, looks at me with curiosity, then asks, "Why are you using Yogananda and not Brahman?"

"It's more difficult with him," I say thoughtfully. "I mean, I think he's wonderful and everything, and I can sense his presence here. I really can. But I don't feel like I really know him." I give her a warm smile.

"It's no problem. You have seen his face, haven't you?" she says and beams at me excitedly. She looks so amazingly happy when she suggests I try using Brahman as my image for the Divine that I can't help believing maybe I should. She seems to be vibrating on a totally different level, so full of love and higher consciousness.

My footsteps are filled with determination as I walk back to the meditation hall. *One way or another, I'm going to master this. If Nicolita can do it, surely can I.*

I decide to give it a fair chance, to see if I can put all of my notions about the Divine into Brahman, and it feels exciting. With a spring in my steps, I almost fly around the corner with excitement before I suddenly remember that I'm on a silent retreat where we are supposed to walk slowly and be contemplative at all times.

I pause to compose myself before entering the meditation hall. As I open the doors, the familiar soft aroma of incense welcomes me. I walk straight through the room and head for the altar. I've seen other people do this before, throughout the retreat, but I've felt too self-conscious to follow their lead. I bow to the picture of Brahman. Then I lie down on my stomach with my head toward the altar, arms outstretched like I've seen others do, and pray for help to turn my image of the Divine into his form. I am doing my best to humble myself.

As I lie there on the ground, I have a silent conversation with Brahman, explaining that I am still finding this very difficult and asking him to please bear with me. In just a few moments, I can feel him standing in front of me. I'm so astounded, I don't know what to make of it all. I tell Brahman how I struggle with feelings of non-belonging and a fear of being rejected. In a paradoxical way, I know this conversation is happening within me, and at the same time it feels good to get everything out in the open. I'm somehow organizing my thoughts and feelings. Before I go back to my mat, I pray for more beautiful energy and insights.

◆◆◆

I don't have to wait long. In the evening, we are blessed with another infinity meditation and it's even more sensational than it was the last time. As the divine beings are meditating at the front of the hall, I allow myself to become the recipient of higher consciousness. The energy of the meditation feels extremely powerful, like it's surrounding me on all sides. It is so intense, in fact, that the whole room suddenly feels like nothingness. It's a paradoxical sensation. I'm floating out in all directions and I have a wonderful sensation of no separation between me and anything around me. I'm everywhere and nowhere. The sensation of floating out of my body is even more powerful and blissful than it was during the meditation on the rainy November night in California.

I suddenly find myself back in my body, aware of myself and my surroundings. I feel light and full of love. All the love I'm feeling brings memories of Richard into my heart, and I can't help smiling.

Richard and I met at a friend's wedding about a year ago. We were with our respective partners. I was there with Michael as it happens, and there was a lot of tension between us that day. Just before coming to the wedding, Michael had told me he doesn't really feel that attracted to me. I was. needless to say, very hurt, and felt lost. The moment Richard and I started talking, I suddenly felt happy again. I was absolutely mesmerized by him. He was so alive and full of passion. All I could think about was how much I wanted to be with a man like him.

No, not just like him . . . him. I remember.

So maybe Michael actually did me a favor meeting another girl. I was stuck in a relationship for way too long where I wasn't happy. It wasn't until we broke up several months later that I began seeing more of Richard. As luck would have it, he and his girlfriend had recently split as well.

Richard is openly spiritual like me. A Buddhist, he wears a golden and red Buddha pendant necklace. As opposed to many of my other friends, when I talk enthusiastically with him about crystals and healing, he's genuinely interested. He seems open to everything. He's an adventurer, for sure. I love being near him.

21.

"Ask for help"

WALKING AROUND HERE at the ashram grounds, looking at everyone meditating, resting, sitting in chairs, or strolling slowly in silence sometimes makes me feel like we're all in a psych ward! Especially since most of us are dressed in white from head to toe. At other moments, however, as I look out of my bedroom window and see the rooftops of the huts in the village, I feel vibrantly alive and grateful to be somewhere so different, almost like I've dropped into the movie *Out of Africa*. I loved the scenery in that movie. Whenever I realize I'm in an exotic place, somewhere very far away from the rest of the Western world, I feel a thrill of excitement and adventure.

Today in class, we're focusing on intention. We get blessings from the dasas filled with intention energy. I can feel a strange sensation spreading through my body. It's on the border of being uncomfortable, but as has been true so many times before, I'm not experiencing discomfort anywhere near the level that many of those around me are demonstrating. Some people are now throwing themselves on the floor, screaming and crying or laughing hysterically, and some are even singing strange sounds. *Who are these people? Why are they acting like this? Are they even real?* I think. The thought that some of them may be actors enters my mind again.

THE   DREAM   ALCHEMIST

I recall a conversation with Nicolita, on the way to the cafeteria one day, in which she told me that some devotees in the room are actually spirits who are here to help us through the process. *Is this what they are? Spirits who are just here to accelerate things by screaming out their pain so that others will feel comfortable doing the same?* I feel perplexed and confused.

On my way to breakfast, after class, I begin to feel nauseous and a bit dizzy. I would love to do some gentle stretch yoga, but I'm not sure my body has the energy for it. I feel anguished. Just as I'm about to step into the cafeteria, I see Nicolita. I hasten my steps to catch up to her. "Nicolita," I say, "Can I ask you something?"

She turns and awaits me patiently. "How can I accept all aspects of myself?" I ask her.

Emanating a wise energy all around, Nicolita responds in a warm tone, "The only way is to ask for it. This is not something you can do with your own effort. You need to ask for help."

Of course! I keep forgetting. The dasas had spoken about this many times before in the meditation hall. Here I am thinking everything is under my control, and what I really need to do is to ask for help and surrender.

Nicolita's words feel comforting and encouraging. I'm not alone, and there is help whenever I need it.

22.

THE BREAKDOWN

AFTER BREAKFAST, I walk back to the dormitory to hang out for a bit, write in my journal, and contemplate on everything I've experienced so far. But I can't write. It hurts too much to reflect on the causes of my suffering. I have real pain in my chest.

Like Nicolita suggested, I try asking Brahman for help to experience my suffering, to feel everything, accept myself, and then surrender. However, it doesn't go the way I planned. By doing so, I intended to let go, feel the light, and be free from it all. Instead my request backfires, and now I'm filled with so much pain all over my body that I can hardly breathe.

I've heard before that in the deepest despair and darkest moments, the energy can be so heavy that it seems like time is standing still. In such moments we are just waiting and have no choice other than to experience who we are and develop full acceptance of all our parts. I guess that is what is happening to me. I'm experiencing real pain and it feels like I'm never going to get out of it.

I need some privacy, away from the dormitory. I walk into the ladies' restroom and close the door to the stall. The pain that's inside me wells up and turns into a deep cry. I don't think I've ever hurt this much. All I ever wanted in my life was to feel like I belonged. Thank goodness I'm here in India. This needs to be healed, and that healing is occurring now.

As I exit the stall and go to wash my hands, a cleaning lady pats me on the arm. "Don't cry," she says tenderly. "It's OK." I feel so grateful to have some human interaction. *She must not care about silent rules,* I think to myself, *and I'm really happy she doesn't.*

Just when I think I can't possibly cry anymore, the meditation session before lunch turns into a three-hour marathon of continuous crying. The dasa leading the group asks us to go back into our childhood and confront our parents about whatever painful moments arise in our minds. First, I can't think of many painful memories, but then a few flashbacks of feeling hurt come before my eyes and my heart beats faster with pain. I want to cry even more. As always, people around me are screaming, calling out their anger and frustration in words. It is starting to feel quite scary. I even have to put my fingers in my ears for a while. These angry people around me are interfering with my process. Then there is more pain, followed by more pain.

We continue, now reflecting upon the pain we've caused others. If the exercise in the morning was hard, thinking about how other people have hurt me . . . well, that was nothing in comparison to the pain I am now feeling. I am breaking down. It's too much. I can't bear it anymore. All I want is to go home. But I know the gates to the property are locked. To leave the grounds, unless it's an organized daytrip somewhere, one would need to experience some kind of medical emergency. I signed papers before coming here that I wouldn't leave until the process was completed. Now I feel like I've signed myself into something very dangerous. *Will I even survive this? I may have a heart attack. There is no way a person with a weak heart would make it through this process.*

I take a deep breath. I know I need to calm down and find my inner peace.

23.

MIRRORS

IT'S AFTERNOON AND the dasa in front of the room is talking about the art of forgiveness. She says, "To forgive a person is to forgive someone for that same aspect of yourself, and to no longer be disturbed by that person." Even though I've heard and read what she's talking about many times before in different contexts, this is the first time I think I'm actually starting to get it. If someone annoys me, there is something the person is doing that reminds me of something I do as well, perhaps without even knowing what it is.

Sometimes it's easy to figure out how our behavior is similar to another person's, but other times finding a comparison can be very confusing, as the characteristics that we share with others, the things we both do, may be done totally unconsciously by us. I may be totally clueless that I'm actually doing something even remotely similar.

The dasa continues, "Not liking a quality in someone reveals there's a charge there. It is because we embody that quality. When we don't like something in somebody, it is really in ourselves that we don't like that quality. We are that person."

I love how the dasas clarify everything so eloquently. Nothing they are saying is new to me. But it feels good to hear them verbalize everything and put it into context while I'm meditating on what they are saying. It brings clarity all around. Or I wonder if it perhaps is because I'm so wiped out and cleansed from all the crying that I can finally take it all in?

After a few minutes of silence and contemplation, the dasa adds, "When we're at peace, there's no need to set anything right or to forgive, as we're already fine."

I taste her words. This feels right. Whatever energy frequency I'm in attracts matching experiences. I manifest situations and people into my life that reflect where I am and the things I need to learn to advance to higher levels. This is the process of higher awareness. If I'm in a place of inner harmony, I don't walk around thinking about things that upset me and I'm less likely to let situations disrupt my harmony.

We meditate some more, and then, as if the dasa in front of the room knows exactly what I've been thinking these last few days, she suddenly breaks the meditation and says, "The only way we can fully accept ourselves and feel like we belong is to feel completely loved." She concludes, "Anything that is fully experienced will blossom into love."

I sit back on my mat, relax, and allow myself to bathe in this loving wisdom. I would love to be filled with love all the time and be fully connected to everything and everyone, wherever I go.

24.

A New Day

WHEN I WOKE up this morning, it felt like I'd spent the night getting banged around inside a coffin, in absolute turmoil, falling rapidly down a waterfall. Funnily enough, that's one of the strange images I had all day yesterday as well. Then, during our morning meditation, the dasa leading the room reminded us to find the Divine in our hearts. I struggled again. Instead of finding a connection, I ended up feeling sadder and emptier, and battling feelings of disbelief. After breakfast, I walked slowly back to the dormitory with immense sadness within me.

I'm now lying here on my bed. If I'm being absolutely honest with myself, I'm actually feeling a little angry for having wasted all this precious time of my life allowing myself to get to this low point, which surely must be rock bottom. *Why in heaven's name am I undergoing this experience voluntarily? Will I ever get out of this low point? How can this possibly be serving my higher good?* I have literally experienced so much pain that I'm beginning to worry about the health of my heart. *My goodness, I'm falling apart.*

I take a sip of water. My water bottle is almost empty, so I go outside in the corridor outside the dormitory and fill it up. There are big containers there with fresh drinking water, which I am very thankful for. A few girls have already become sick, and one even has had to be put on antibiotics. I feel very lucky to be healthy at least. And what's more, I'm glad I haven't been chased by a monkey! I walk back into my room and pick up my journal.

I'm going over the beautiful teachings from the meditation room, which advise us to stay with whatever we're feeling so we may fully experience any sensations that may arise. To stay with this dark energy and the sad feelings is not hard at this point, I'm entangled in them. What I want is to find a way out.

I remember one of the dasas saying we need to pray for help. If so, then it's clear that nothing is going to happen until I am able to build a relationship with the Divine. I need to do it fast, so that I can pray effectively for help to be released from this entrapment. I pray that I'll be able to pray and set free. I pray every second on my way to lunch, during lunch, and after lunch. I pray to feel better, to feel loved, and to feel like I belong wherever I go.

◆◆◆

In the afternoon, we continue meditating. For the first time since I began experiencing heavy sadness, I feel myself letting go. I just can't fight it anymore. It's time to surrender. Within a few seconds of me thinking those words, the most miraculous thing happens. There is a powerful shift in the room. The dasa suddenly stands up. With a joyful tone in her voice she says, "Let's pray for love to fill us completely." She pauses for almost a minute, and then adds, "And for the child to awaken within us!"

Following the sound of the dasa's last word, an incredible energy begins flowing into the top of my head from above and surrounds me from every direction! I feel like a child again, and I can see myself back at my dad's house in the country, dressed in white.

We are asked to stand up and I can sense that something truly amazing is about to happen. The air is charged with electricity. Then it happens. The sound of music fills the room—and it's not Indian chanting. Nor is it sacred sounds from the tanpura or the esraj, the stringed instruments we've been hearing so much of. It is Enya. Enya! Her beautiful song "A New Day" fills the room and I am flooded with happy tears! This is not only my first connection with the Western world since arriving here, but even more so, my first real contact with the outer world, apart from my brief interaction with the Spanish helper who was playing a few slow strums on the guitar the other night, and being comforted by the cleaning woman in the restroom. This feels like a whole different level of connection. It is the first happy song I've heard since arriving here, and I'm no longer stuck inside my head feeling pain.

We all must be sharing pretty similar feelings, because everyone around me is now standing up, smiling, and radiating joy. If a stranger walked through the door, he'd probably think we've just been granted the wishes of our lives. Everyone spontaneously dances around the room and I begin moving to the music like I have wings. I move around the room with the grace of an angel.

I've always liked this song, but never really felt it before. It's truly amazing. Who knew how powerful Enya could be? I doubt I can ever love another song the way I love this one right now. This is one of the most blissful moments I've ever experienced. *The suffering has ended. I made it through. I am alive.*

When I get back to the dormitory, I open the little drawer next to my bed where I am keeping my journal, phone, camera, and wallet. I sit down and power up my phone for the first time since I got here. First, I send a quick text to my mom saying I'm OK and that I'm having a great time. Then I take a deep breath and start writing a text to Michael:

> *I am at an ashram in India on a meditation retreat. After a week in emotional torture it has finally dawned on me that it was my own negative life patterns that trigged your uncertainties in our relationship. I forgive you. You are now free to love. This place is blessed with divine energy and I am so touched to be here.*
> *Namaste*

25.

DREAMS

THE NEXT DAY turns out to be extraordinary beyond measure. In the afternoon, we have another infinity meditation with enlightened beings in front of the room. During the meditation, my thoughts drift a bit. I experiment with viewing my thoughts as if they're on a movie screen, trying to push them in front of my forehead. First it feels like they have assumed the form of the Great Wall of China, then somehow they take on a triangular shape.

Even though I'm not fully engaged with my thoughts, I still feel immensely distracted, so I try pushing them slightly upward, followed by pushing them straight up—and there it is! My whole head feels like it has opened up like a lotus flower!

I'm floating around in a golden energy field for the longest time, and all I feel is peace. I suddenly snap back into the room when I hear one of the dasas say, "It's all a dream. We are dreaming. The world itself is a dream where we all play parts and have been given free will to create our own dreams. We're all dreaming together."

I feel a big rush of excitement, this is what I've been feeling and knowing all along! We are dreaming a highly lucid dream, which feels exceptionally real, and somehow we're all in it together. How it works, I have no idea, but I sure hope to find out one day.

I am a dreamer. This is what I'm here on Earth to do: to learn about dreams, embark on dream adventures, and share dream journeys. Life is all a dream.

The inspiration I'm feeling is something out of this world. Seated in the cafeteria at dinner, feeling a spiritual high beyond measures, I suddenly notice one of the western helpers standing next to me, giving me a warm smile. She asks, "Would you be able to participate in the homa on Saturday, which will be broadcasted in Sweden?" She then looks at me with so much joy and expectation.

I meet her eyes with a mixture of excitement and confusion. "Well, I'm not sure. I'm new here," I respond brightly. I can't help feeling a rush of energy from speaking to someone and actually being acknowledged.

She gives a warm laugh. "I must have got you totally confused, I thought you had been here longer. I apologize for breaking your silence!"

I must be radiating my bliss in all directions, because just a few minutes later another girl approaches me and asks me if I am a helper.

This is a new day in all kinds of ways, and I'm loving every moment of it.

26.

PERCEPTIONS

EVERY DAY IN our sessions with the dasas we're reminded to observe our thoughts, breath, and emotions. This is a good exercise. After all, the most profound insight came to Buddha just from observing and being in this in-between state where he was simply not trying anything too hard. Every now and then, I manage to float away and just observe, which is an amazing feeling. Sometimes I struggle more; thoughts swirl around in my head. At the end of the day, this meditation technique is all about being in a state of observation and being aware of our perception. This applies to suffering as well.

The dasas often talk about how it is our perception of what is happening to us that makes us suffer. Losing money is not suffering itself. Suffering comes from what we think of it, from our own painful interpretation of events. We can try to change our perception, but it won't really change until we have reached higher consciousness. Reaching a higher level of consciousness enables us to gain a new perspective that transcends pain.

Changing our perception is easier said than done however. I've tried many times before and been unsuccessful. It may work for a couple of hours, but then it's so easy to snap back into old reactions to events. I guess that's why we first need to work on our consciousness!

It's now 8:00 p.m. and I'm waiting to meet with Nicolita. I love our sacred meetings because on top of the wisdom she shares with me, I also get to talk with another human being! A heavily built girl comes out of the room, and I walk in.

As I sit down next to Nicolita on the brown sofa, and look into her big, brown eyes, I wonder how she can possibly look so serene all the time. I ask her, "What am I to do about my unhealthy relationship patterns? I somehow always seem to end up with a man who is seeing other women and this makes me feel jealous and hurt. Should I avoid situations that are more jealous prone, or just accept that jealousy is part of life?"

Nicolita looks peacefully at me. As she places her hands on mine, she says, "The answer is not to avoid jealousy or to go for less jealousy. When you accept that jealousy is a beautiful state in itself, you can be with whomever you want and be happy!"

27.

A Loving Benediction

IT'S A SUNNY Indian morning and the exotic sounds of birds and bugs can be heard all over the ashram grounds. Today is a special day. We're going to an ancient temple located on sacred grounds.

I am standing outside my dormitory, next to all the other silent devotees, awaiting buses to take us to the temple. Once onboard the bus, I feel an immense thrill of excitement at seeing all the village people we pass on the road. I can't believe I'm here in South India in the middle of the countryside on an old bus going through a village filled with women in colorful sarongs, men selling coconuts, and children playing on the streets. I am an intrepid soul and this kind of travel is the life I was meant to live. Being out in the world, having soul adventures! I take a deep breath and let India live inside me. I never want to forget this journey.

As we pull in closer to the temple grounds, I have to catch my breath. It's enormous, bigger than any temple I've ever seen. I don't think I have to worry about not remembering this moment. The temple is spectacular, like something out of the legend of Atlantis. I step out of the bus and see monkeys sitting on one of the walls next to the temple. I try my best not to meet their casual, but slightly intense gazes, and walk up the white marble temple steps with mixed feelings of novelty, curiosity, and an inner sense of already knowing where I'm going. The whole group makes its way into the middle of the temple and forms a big circle. From the corners of my eyes, I see monkeys observing us closely through the open windows.

We chant for what feels like an hour, but could be less. At the end of the chant, I feel very excited to stand up and do something new. The dasa leads us all into a big meditation space, and I notice a picture of Brahman in the front of the room. She tells us we're here to receive a sacred benediction!

We chant Brahman's mantra three times to invoke the divine presence. Some people have already gone up to the picture and placed their hands on it. As I sit here waiting for my turn, I can't help feeling a little perplexed. *Why are we receiving a blessing from a picture? Am I never going to meet Brahman in person?* The dasas have told us several times how Brahman's energy can be found in his pictures, but I'm having a hard time accepting this. I still feel excited though. The energy is high and people are so full of devotion that's it's just wonderfully contagious.

When it's my turn to receive the blessing, my whole body begins shaking. *Where is all this anxiety coming from? Now I'm feeling intimidated by a picture?!* I slowly sit down and tentatively place my hand on Brahman's hand in the picture. I take a deep breath, relax, and then it happens. I feel it. *I'm not just imagining this. I can really feel it. There's energy flowing through me.* This is probably the first time that I haven't worried about taking up somebody else's time. As opposed to how I received the other blessings from the elderly dasas who were enlightened, this time I do not rush through and allow myself just to feel it. I know that I deserve to be here as much as anybody else in the room. This is my journey. I stay in front of the picture until I feel the energy slow down, then I make my way to the back of the room and lay down on the floor. Around me there are quite a lot of other devotees doing the same.

As I lie there, I pray for the highest level of consciousness my body can handle right now, and for more to come as soon as I'm ready. I am in a state of ecstasy and bliss, and find myself floating in and out of my body. I wonder how I got to this frequency. *Was it really through the picture? Or was it the anticipation that something amazing was about to happen to me, that allowed me to fully let go?* However I got here, this is very powerful.

I don't know how long I've been lying on the floor, it may be hours. It's surreal and serene at the same time, and very funny. The vision I have right now is of getting married to God. This is my wedding day inside a gorgeous Atlantean temple!

28.

NAVAYA

OH MY STARS, we've just found out that we'll be meeting with an amazing sacred woman called Navaya tomorrow morning. Navaya is one of Brahman's closest disciples, and the dasas told us we can wish for something directly from our hearts.

I feel happy and full of anticipation, although there is a small part of me that fears I may not be able to fully connect with her. What if everyone becomes a devotee but me? I'm only just tentatively beginning to develop a special bond with Brahman. How can I now also put my notion of the Divine into the form of one of Brahman's disciples? I feel confusion slowly spreading through my body. *What if I come back from India, and nothing has happened to me? Then I've wasted all this time and people will feel sorry for me.*

I enter the meditation hall where a lot of devotees have gathered to prepare a song to share with Navaya tomorrow. I sit down next to a girl with long hair. "I can't believe we can talk tonight. How amazing is this!" I say to her.

With a peaceful, angelic look in her eyes, she turns to me and says, "Yes, this is one of the most magical times ever. This is the real deal. It's happening now. All our hard work has prepared us for this moment."

I smile and can't help feeling excitement. *Maybe I am turning into a devotee after all? Maybe I'm not so different from the others?*

It feels so fun to be able to talk for a while and share the joy that so many people are obviously feeling. Just a few minutes after singing together, my happiness comes back. *OK, I know I can do this. I'm meeting with Navaya tomorrow. Yippee!*

◆◆◆

It's afternoon and we're finally on our way back to the ancient temple to meet with Navaya. Once we get there, I walk around the celestial temple grounds, waiting for the main doors to open. People are starting to line up and I join what now feels like a line of excited fans ready to enter a rock concert. As soon as the doors open, everyone rushes to the front of the room. There are two devotees here at the retreat who always rush to take the front row whatever we're doing or wherever we go, and sure enough, there they are again, sitting in the front row. I grab a seat somewhere in the middle.

The back door opens and in walks Navaya. Dressed in a beige dress with light scarves flowing all around her, she truly looks like a divine mother. The air is charged. It's so silent in the room that you could hear a pin drop. She sits down and slowly gazes around the room for a few seconds. My heart takes a little jolt when our eyes meet. Although she isn't smiling, she has a beautiful presence and I can feel her warmth in my chest.

As we begin singing the song we have prepared, I meet her eyes once more. Then she closes her eyes and takes in our gift. The joy of offering a song to her makes me smile with my whole heart. I love this feeling so much. *Maybe I should sing more when I go home!* When our song is done, she reaches out her hands to us and blesses us. *What an experience!* As she leaves, we all lay down on the floor to meditate in a timeless field of divine energy.

29.

THE PREMONITION

SOMETHING REALLY INTERESTING happened to me last night. I woke up in a very strange state. It was so foreign to me that I even had to double check I was, in fact, still breathing. It felt as if my upper body and head were open and directly connected to a golden field around and above me. I became aware of feeling with my whole heart. It felt wonderful. I was floating in infinite love.

As I lie in bed this morning, stretching out so softly, a dream slowly comes back to me. I take out my journal and record whatever I can remember from my dream adventure:

A group of devotees and I are on a bus together, driving out in the countryside. We enter a narrow road on a high and steep mountain, and suddenly the bus falls down the cliff. Just as we're about to crash on the ground, I remind everyone this is just a dream and we're fine.

As I write, I can't help feeling amazed how I could have felt so calm in the dream. I would normally have panicked in such a situation, yet I was sure everything would be OK. It was a good dream. The journey I'm on may be a bit hard for me, and I may already have fallen down, or perhaps I'm about to, but all is well. *I need to remember this the next time I feel afraid.*

In the afternoon, the dasa leading class talks about how there is only one mind. She says we all experience the same feelings in different situations. I can't help feeling particularly touched by hearing these words today. It's so beautiful. I know it's true. We share the same feelings: The fear, the anger, the worry, the love, the joy is the same whether you're a child in Sweden or the president of the United States. I'm finally beginning to understand what it means when people say we're all one.

Ultimately, freedom from anger, anxiety, fear, and worry does not come from trying to escape our feelings, but from embracing them and accepting them as parts of us. After all, if all our feelings are the same, there's no escape anyway. The experience of loving all our feelings itself turns the feelings to joy.

It's now nighttime. I'm lying in bed thinking about my experiences here at the retreat. I keep having amazing insights, but I'm conflicted at the same time. There's a part of me that really wants nothing more than to reach higher awareness and understand how everything really is, but another part just wants to keep things the way they are and doesn't want to let go of the old me. I'm beginning to feel exceptionally sleepy and drift off to dreamland sooner than I can close my eyes.

30.

SOMEWHERE IN TIME

WHEN I WAKE up I hear what sounds like tinkling fairy bell sounds somewhere in the background. Where is this angelic sound coming from? Early in the retreat, I purchased a white silk scarf blessed by Navaya, and I'm now sleeping under it, using it as a mosquito net. It's strange, but it almost feels as if the sound is coming from the scarf itself! My head feels clear, like crystalline glass. I open my eyes, but despite feeling so much clarity I have no idea of where I am. I could be anywhere, at any point in time. It's not like I don't know if I'm in California, Sweden, London, Sydney, or anywhere I've lived before. I don't even know who I am. It takes me a few seconds to collect myself and come back fully into my body. What an interesting way to wake up!

It's perhaps even more curious that I would wake up feeling I could be anywhere at any point in time, because in the meditation hall after breakfast the dasas are talking about how we're all volumes of stories that have happened to us in some point in time.

Time is one of the wonders of life. For the longest time I thought I was the only one walking around pondering on this subject. When I realized it's also considered one of the biggest mysteries of the scientific world, I was thrilled beyond belief.

I suddenly hear the dasa say, "Once a story empties itself, it's free of emotional charge." I wonder how much I've missed of her words. *Oh my. I'm somewhere else today.* I close my eyes and pray for help with feeling my stories so I can let go of the ones that no longer serve me.

◆◆◆

I'm feeling particularly peaceful and content all day. After lunch I walk down through the open grounds to the meditation hall with Nicolita. I seize the opportunity to speak with her, since she's one of the few people I'm actually allowed to talk to. I ask her, "How is it that some people feel more worried and have more negative thoughts than others? If we all have the same mind, how can this be?"

She stops for a second, looks at me with her serene eyes, and then answers, "It all depends on how we grew up. Like antennas, some people will attract certain thoughts more than others. Unresolved emotions are full of charge, so they attract more thoughts." With a twinkle in her eyes, she adds, "Don't be afraid to lose control; the truth is you've never been in control." Then she smiles, nods, and continues walking.

I enter the meditation hall and I hear her words ringing in my ears. I feel like laughing over my own silly need to master my feelings and always be in control. How could she possibly have known this?

In today's discussion after our meditation session, the dasas talk about *vastu,* the ancient Vedic art of balancing elements through placement and energy flow. I must admit I'm feeling confused. If vastu is a way to set up our homes and environments to surround ourselves with good energy, then wouldn't it be best to avoid certain places and people? I raise my hand to ask for clarity.

A dasa at the front of the room answers, "When your heart is blossoming and you awaken to higher realities, none of the bad energy around you matters. These are some external measures you can utilize to make your process of awakening easier. But there is no need to stay away from places or people when your heart is blossoming."

Hmm, so vastu is helpful while we're developing higher aware-ness, but once we've reached a higher state of consciousness, that no longer matters? It's all so confusing. I feel I'm receiving many double messages, but I also know it all comes down to the fact that I'm not there yet, not blossoming, and I won't understand it until I get there.

31.

FREEDOM WITH ALL OUR PERSONALITIES

IN THE MEDITATION room this morning we are being asked to confront our doubts. The dasa is telling us about her first spiritual experience, as a fourteen-year-old girl. She explains how there was a sudden light in her room and then a spiritual being looked her straight in the eyes. As I listen to her telling her story, my thoughts drift off to my own encounters with spiritual beings, such as the love-filled visitation by the little fairy I saw a few months ago. I find it interesting that such visions for me typically occur when I've been feeling down.

My attention goes back to the dasa, and I hear her say, "I felt sad and helpless that night, so I had asked the Divine why I never see any signs." Her words remind me that the fairy showed up after I wished with all my heart for something special to happen to me. I was asking God for something extraordinary and got a bigger sign than I ever could have imagined.

Wow! There must be something to this. There really is someone listening. Before our powerful visions, both me and the dasa had made a wish straight from our hearts, and we got a response!

◆◆◆

Chakra is a Sanskrit word that means "wheel." We have seven major chakra energy "wheels" in our bodies. Our chakras have energy fields spinning like vortexes, and they each vibrate at a different frequency. If we're feeling tired or ill, the chakras could be out of alignment or unbalanced. They can be revitalized through meditation. By sending our chakras divine love and light, we align and balance our whole energy field.

That is what we are doing after lunch today. We are now meditating on our crown chakra, which is located on top of the head. I'm having a hard time concentrating, and my thoughts drift back to a conversation I had with Nicolita about how to discern between my own internal voice and the voice of the Divine. She told me love is the answer. Whenever an experience fills us with ultimate love, we can know it's divine guidance and not just the mind talking.

The meditation is powerful. Once more, I sense a golden light spreading around me. In the midst of it, it strikes me how all the visions I've had throughout my life could well be glimpses of a higher plane of reality, and this may indeed be the consciousness that I need to awaken for everything to make sense. By spending more time immersed in the new higher frequency of the golden light, I will hopefully be able to see this plane of existence which exists simultaneously with ours.

Suddenly Nicolita stands up in front of the class and says, "We're all made up of different personalities. Life itself is learning to live with these personalities. Some of our personalities have negative charges, and those are the ones we need to watch out for. Before we can process whatever conflict is going on, the negative personalities need to be cleansed of their negative charges. Personalities are always arguing for their own stories, so they're in a constant fight."

I very much hope my negative personalities are being cleansed of negative charges while I'm here at the retreat, and that I can learn to live in harmony. I know it's true. I will never have freedom *from* my personalities, I will only have freedom *with* them. But in order for that to happen, they need to be free of emotional charge. That is, of course, the answer!

All this time, I have been wondering how I could ever become free when there is so much dissonance going on inside my mind. That is probably one of the reasons we're meditating so much while we're here. Before anything can happen, the emotional charges in us need to be neutralized. I close my eyes and pray for all the negative charges inside my personalities to be removed and for my positive personalities to take the forefront.

The dasa softly adds, "Remember to continue praying as any negative thoughts occur. You may think you are one absolute person. You are not! We are all made up of various personalities."

32.

"PEOPLE ARE NOT WHO WE THINK THEY ARE"

WHEN I WAKE up, the first thing I recall is a dream from last night:

> I'm pregnant, and I have a big, hard stomach. I go for an ultrasound, and the lady tells me the baby could arrive any minute, any day. I am contemplating whether to do a cesarean or have a natural birth. I'm not sure how the baby comes out in the end, but once he's born, I hold him for only a few seconds and then hand him to someone else. A few minutes later, I suddenly realize I'm not holding him, and take him back. He says, "More milk."

There's definitely something evolving inside me, namely my consciousness, which could be symbolized by the baby in the dream! I find it interesting how I first give the baby to someone else to hold, but then realize I need to hold him myself, and that the baby needs milk. If the baby represents the spiritual awakening growing inside me, it's clearly important that I nourish and love myself more.

The night before last, I had another interesting dream. As I reread the entry for it in my journal, a couple of lines jump off the page at me.

> *I am bicycling, and feel very excited to remember this skill. I am bicycling with my top off, and have no bra on, and I feel so confident!*

Ha ha, I reflect, *this probably has to do with me feeling very balanced here at the spiritual retreat, and remembering a skill I haven't used since childhood. Also, the dream is an acknowledgment that I have no problem showing the world my true self. I'm comfortable in my own body. In fact, I'm naked and exposed on many levels here at the ashram, and I'm feeling very contented.*

My dream life is becoming an important part of my transformational process.

I'm feeling pretty good today. But there's still much I'm trying to make sense of. On my way back to class after lunch, I see Nicolita walking in front of me. I accelerate my pace to catch up to her. Then I say, "I can't help wondering, if feelings are not my own, then how can I know if a fairy I saw once was real? I felt incredible love when I saw her. It was so amazing, she was radiating with it." I told Nicolita about the visitation a few days ago.

Nicolita looks at me tenderly, "You already answered your own question. You're telling me how you were feeling when you saw the fairy, that pure love was spreading throughout your body. This is awakening. There is no 'fully awakened' state. Awakening is a process.

"As for the other visions you've had in your life, those were not ghosts. To put this in your own words, they were glimpses of another reality with messages from God. Divine beings are all around us, even in the world here at the ashram. There are even divine beings in the meditation hall who are here to help us. People are not who you think they are." I knew it!

I get to speak with Nicolita a lot today. We meet in the lounge in the evening as well. After I tell her of my desire to immerse myself in higher consciousness, she asks me, "Are you wondering about your career? Remember that you need to work! It is important that you do what excites and interests you, and that you do something that will feel better in your heart. It needs to be something that helps the world."

Hmm. I wonder, *maybe it's time to change my career.*

It's funny to give myself permission to consider the possibilities. There's such a sense of freedom! When I return to the dormitory, I take out my journal and begin jotting down things I can say I truly enjoy in life. It turns into quite a long list. There's a lot of things I love doing. *I had better keep this list handy for a rainy day,* I think. *When the darkness hits, it's not always easy to remember what makes us happy.*

MY FAVORITE THINGS
Reading
Walking on the beach
Dancing
Listening to music
Playing music
Singing
Writing
Dreaming
Cooking for someone
Going for dinner at a nice restaurant
Dressing up nicely
Traveling to places with an exotic feel
Staying in nice hotels
Having breakfast by the hotel pool/ocean
Drinking red wine
Hugging animals
Loving somebody
Visiting beautiful nature/scenic places/rainforests
Visiting historical landmarks
Waterfalls
Feeling energy fields
Yoga
Crystals
Decorating the house

Flowers
Beautiful fragrances and creams
Channeling energy
Feeling good
Being open, with chest/heart chakra flourishing
Going to concerts
Grocery shopping in a beautiful store
Thinking and contemplating
Making people feel good
Holding presentations when I feel confident
Entertaining
Connecting people

33.

A DREAMY LIFE

THROUGHOUT MY ENTIRE life, two activities close to my heart that have brought me inspiration and an inner source of excitement and fascination are writing and dreaming. As a thirteen-year-old in Sweden, my literature teacher started becoming more and more intrigued with my writing. When he found out one day that I was receiving most of my inspiration from my dream world, he excitedly told me, "Anna-Karin, you are a very gifted and talented writer for such a young age, and now you tell me you're getting your inspiration from your dreams. You really need to read Freud this instant!"

I remember riding my blue bicycle down to our modest-sized town library that same day. On one of the shelves in the back corner, I found a dusty old copy of the book *Dream Interpretation* by Sigmund Freud. It had a red cover. As young as I was, I dove into the pages of the book and felt genuinely happy to know that there were other people who also wondered about the meaning of their dreams. It was not just me. After having devoured this first book, I threw myself into reading as many other dream books as I could find, which was not an easy task in our little town. If I found a new one in a store I would buy it. Over time, I managed to build up a small personal dream book library.

It would be many years before I was introduced to the Swizz Psychiatrist Carl Jung. I'm not sure if reading Freud before Jung was the best way for me to go, but that was the way my life panned out. Perhaps I just wasn't ready for Jung's more spiritual approach yet. Freud and Jung differ quite a lot in their approaches to dream work and their understanding of the un- conscious mind. Whereas Freud was only interested in a per- son's individual unconscious, Jung was also interested in the collective unconscious of humanity. Jung described this as a field shared by all living people, a field we all tap into when we dream.[1]

Jung's spiritual approach to dreams is the reason, no doubt, that I feel more drawn to his teachings. A lot of the work we are doing in our sessions with the dasas reminds me about teach- ings in Jungian psychology. In the Jungian school of thought, a big part of working on ourselves includes bringing our shadow selves to the surface. The shadow is composed of the aspect of us that we have repressed because we don't feel comfortable with it. Whereas other people often see our shadow demonstrat- ed through our actions, we are usually oblivious to our own shadow natures. It is only by observing ourselves closely that we can learn about the nature of our own shadows.

Even though the dasas often urge us to get to know all our personalities and do our best to accept them, I find it interest- ing how they don't talk much about dream work. By looking at characters that show up in our dreams we can learn a lot about our hidden personalities, and that is a powerful way of bringing our shadow out.

I have wondered a lot about my hidden personalities these last few days. When I look back upon my relationship patterns there is clearly a girl inside me who puts up with situations that are not healthy, pleasing others because she so wishes to be loved and feel like she belongs. She keeps giving more and more of herself, hoping it will work out if she just tries harder. *That may be one of my shadow personalities,* I think. *Maybe there is a part of me that is afraid of not belonging, and even feels rejected?*

34.

A DREAM MEETING

MY DREAMS ARE becoming more and more vivid every day now. This morning I woke up from another intense dream, in which Brahman showed up. It was one of the most real dreams I've ever had. It truly felt like I met him. Somewhere in time, in some realm, this meeting actually took place, I know it. Still lying in bed, I pull out my pen and write it down.

> *I am walking toward our group meeting and all the meditation halls look very different than usual. I am trying to find where we will be meeting, so I'm asking for directions. Suddenly, I hear someone saying that there are three more years for us here if we want to stay for a private course with Brahman, but we have to want to be here with all our hearts. I am sitting down, peeking in through a door. I can see Brahman inside teaching. He sees me and comes toward me. I immediately stand up and greet him with an open heart as he comes closer. We embrace and I tell him how much I would love to stay here close to him, but that I can't be away that long from my family. He smiles, then takes a small step back and I feel desperate. I don't want to let go of him. I want to see him, fully, and feel him, so that I can remember him in my heart forever. I keep on touching his blue tee-shirt with a gray pattern on it, and there is so much love between us.*

*I can tell there is something very different about him. Within his
eyes, I can see divine golden fields.*

It's so interesting that Brahman would come to me in a
dream. The love I experienced standing next to him was out of
this world.

◆◆◆

The whole day today love is in the air. Even before we begin the
morning session, I am walking around vibrating at some kind
of ultimate love frequency, as if I'm floating out in all directions,
feeling incredible love for everyone and everything around me.

In the morning lecture session, a dasa again talks about how
we really have no control. We have no control of body, mind,
thoughts, or personality. She says, "We think we are in control,
and continuously resist giving up control. But the truth is we
have no control of anything, and that is why we are suffering.
We simply have the wrong idea of freedom. Freedom is not being
in control. Freedom is the ability to see whatever is happening."

Then she tells the story of when Buddha first realized he
didn't have to do anything and ended up laughing for days and
nights. With love in her voice, the dasa slowly says, "Experience
life and relax. When you are embraced by love and compassion,
when you surrender and give up, you are empowered to explore
total freedom, love, and joy."

Her words are powerful, and what she's saying rings true to
my ear. All we need to do is to experience and feel love. One of
the dasas is guiding us into a meditation, helping us to pray for
love to be our path, to surrender, and to leave control with the
Divine. As I'm sitting here, in this field of love, it's all starting to
come together. This is, of course, why Brahman appeared in my
dream last night and made me to feel so much love. He came to
help me walk the path of love. He opened the golden gates and
I'm now in angelic euphoria. There is love all around, and would
you believe, the first thing we talk about in class today is love?
Isn't that lovely!

35.

MAUNA ENDS

THE MAUNA HAS now officially come to an end and we are allowed to speak to one another—that is, if we feel like it. I'm actually not sure I even need to talk that much anymore. However, I can sense the love growing between us all as we connect on a new level with eye contact, hugs, and words.

When we were first told that mauna was over, it felt absolutely amazing; it was wonderful to be able to connect with the people I've seen around me for so long, but who have not seemed more substantial to me than clouds on the horizon. Among other things, I am enjoying looking them in the eye. At the same time though, the shock of the difference between having been exclusively focused within myself and opening up my energy field to everyone around me is almost overwhelming. I am determined to be a lot more selective about whom I talk with from now on. Silence is precious. I don't want to break it with just anyone for the sake of talking.

On this love-filled day, apparently others are noticing the love as much as I am. Everyone looks so happy. I'm now sitting on the lawn outside the dormitories, writing in my journal and feeling my aliveness. A man from southern Sweden sits down opposite me.

"This has been quite a journey, eh? How have you found the process, has it been hard on you?" he asks me.

"Oh, definitely," I say. "This has been one of the hardest times of my life. So much pain and hardship. But now, oh my goodness, there is just so much love. I guess we had to go through it all to get here!" Then I laugh.

"It wasn't that hard on me—not this time around," he says. "I've been attending similar retreats in Sweden for a couple of years, so I already went through most of what you guys went through now. It was much harder on me when I first began this self-work."

During lunch, I sit down next to a man from Arizona. He's appears to be in his sixties and looks intriguing. He has penetrating eyes. He tells me he is a psychotherapist and also treats people with energy medicine. It's so much fun to have all these people around me come to life and at least learn more about them. Anyone who works a lot on themselves in my eyes is a soul searcher, and I love hearing their insights from the retreat. With each person I connect with today, I feel myself opening up more and more. I can sense infinite love flowing out of me.

In the afternoon session, we are reminded not to crave permanent states, including states of higher spiritual feelings, or even enlightenment. Hearing this advice, it dawned on me that I might never be able to escape such thoughts. I just need to realize they are there, accept them, and let them be. As I've learned from working with negative states that I formerly rejected, the key is to build on my personal relationship with the Divine and see myself as separate from my thoughts, and view them as a movie. I am not my thoughts.

◆◆◆

Tonight will be a special night. We'll be meeting Brahman to receive sacred *darshan* (personally transmitted energy) from being in his presence. If someone had told me earlier in the retreat that I would be receiving a blessing from Brahman in person, I would probably just have thought, *That sounds nice,* and not made much more of it. As opposed to many others who have made their ways here, I did not come here because of Brahman. I came here to spend some time at an ashram in India and connect with heavenly energies. Little did I know I would come to form a sacred bond with the guru.

36.

"PLEASE SEE ME"

IN THE WESTERN world, the word *guru* still makes some people uncomfortable. It is becoming more accepted to have a guru, but the word itself sometimes brings up associations with cults and mind manipulation. If I'm honest, some of those stigmas used to reside within me as well.

When I was a little girl, a friend of my family became a devotional follower of a guru in Northern India. One day he began dressing in purple and wearing a mala with a picture of his guru around his neck. I remember my family embracing him with warmth and understanding, but there was also an underlying awkwardness whenever he came by after that. I could feel my parents' hesitation whenever they would talk about his transformation from "regular Lenny" into "devotional Leonard." As time went by, they eventually stopped having him over to the house. I always thought this was their choice, but who knows, maybe he found some "more evolved" people to spend time with!

In India, gurus are ever present and looked upon as a routine aspect of spiritual growth. The relationship between guru and devotee is definitely much more accepted here. To have a guru is considered nothing bizarre, it's simply part of the path.

In my own search for enlightenment, holiness, and infinite divinity, I did not know I was looking for a guru, and definitely didn't consciously travel here to become a devotee of Brahman. I don't even know fully how Brahman has taken this large role in my life. I haven't even been here for three weeks yet. Maybe spending so much time in silence within myself has something to do with it, because it feels like I've been here for a lifetime. The way my heart opened to Brahman in the special dream was incredible beyond words.

There is a part inside that just knows I want to have him as my guru. There is no other way. My whole soul is excited to call him *my guru.*

Brahman walks into the meditation hall with his eyes closed, and to my astonishment they remain closed! I want to meet his gaze and be noticed by him. *Please see me*, I think. The moment I think those words something extraordinary happens. He opens his eyes, but he does not look out over the group of people or meet anyone else's eyes, he only looks into mine. He is staring right at me, and not in a dreamy way—but with his eyes wide open. He makes a funny face at me that ends with a little nose wrinkle, then closes his eyes again.

I am in a state of wonder. This did not just happen by chance. What a synchronicity! The second I was thinking of how much I wanted Brahman to look at me, he did - and then closed his eyes again! It was the instant collaboration of my inner and outer worlds. Carl Jung would have loved this story!

I close my eyes and feel love all over my body. One of the dasas asks us to pray for awakening and for our benediction to be to awakened to a connection with everything and everyone around us. I pray with my whole heart. After the darshan ceremony, Brahman stands up and smiles, then walks out. This is an event I will cherish forever. That I am sure of! In this moment, I am one with the Divine. There is a pure, ever-flowing expression of divine consciousness within me.

Back at the ashram, having dinner in the cafeteria, I'm sitting with the psychotherapist from Arizona that I was talking with at lunch yesterday. He leans close to me, and says, "That was an interesting expression Brahman gave you. I saw him look straight at you and make a very funny face."

Now how amazing is this! It was not in my imagination. Brahman really did look at me, because other people noticed!

The truth is, I'm still just a little girl inside, one who often doesn't feel as if she belongs and believes she's not as important as other people. Brahman somehow knew this and gave me the recognition I so wished for.

The man seated next to me may have been asked by the Divine to step in as well, to help me feel thoroughly recognized. Who knows, maybe he is a divine being himself! Didn't Nicolita say that not everyone here is who or what they seem to be?

37.

A Loving Conversation

WE'VE JUST RETURNED to the ashram after receiving a second benediction at the big temple. Now it's midmorning. I'm lying in the green grass and gazing up at the clouds in the sky, and I feel very good about life. All of a sudden, I notice something peculiar. A few people are being followed around by dogs. I guess they must have food in their hands.

The dogs are wild and carry diseases, and we've been warned not to approach them, as they sometimes attack people if they don't get fed. Even though the people being pursued look scared and uncomfortable, I can't help feeling amused by their predicament.

How I can take so much delight in their distress is a mystery. It's so out of character for me. Somehow I just know they'll be safe.

Being here on the grass reminds me of the evening I met the handsome Spanish helper playing the guitar in beginning of the retreat. I've heard other helpers calling him Enrique. There's no doubt about it. I felt a strong attraction to him. I close my eyes and pray with all my heart that I'll get to spend some time alone with him today. I head back inside the dormitory to put my journal away by my bed. It's almost lunchtime and I'm beginning to get hungry. All the love and good feelings have made me appreciate the food here even more. Everything tastes absolutely delicious.

With joy and happiness in my stride, I walk casually down the steps outside the girls' dormitory. In the corner of my eye, I see Enrique emerging from the men's building. Our eyes meet, and the pull is magnetic. We walk closely together, side by side all the way down to the cafeteria.

"I feel so excited," I tell him. "It hasn't happened to me yet, but I'm beginning to see that it's possible not to be involved in negative thoughts. We can step out of them!"

"Oh yes," he says. Once again his Spanish accent sounds so warm and loving. "For sure, it is possible. It's all a process. For me it took about six months. Everything will change you know, when you go home. Your whole life will change."

"Wow," I say. "I'm so ready for that! Are you a devotee of Brahman in Spain?" I ask him.

"Yes, I help people experience divine connection pretty much full time now," he says. "I teach and I organize trips, and then I come back here, to India. What do you do for a living?"

"I'm in the jet industry," I tell him. "But I would really like to do something more for humanity, to help people and do something for the world, you know? Last year I started doing crystal healing and chakra balancing on the side, which I love."

"Ah, so you're one of those who can feel energy fields?" he asks me.

"Yes," I say. That I sure can!

With a loving tone in his voice, he says, "That may be why you are here, you know." He turns to me and with his big, brown eyes looking straight at me, he says, "Buen apetito," and then walks off in the direction of the Spanish table.

Even though I'm amazed we walked out of the two buildings at the same time and got to walk down to lunch together, just as I had been wishing for, I can't help detecting a small negative thought somewhere in the corner of my mind. *What if he doesn't like me?*

After lunch, I walk back to my dorm room, where I pray to be able to feel the separation from my mind on an ongoing basis and not to let myself identify with negative thoughts, but instead just watch them like a movie rolling by. I want to be able to use my mind more like a tool, calling upon its services whenever needed, and for my ideas to be born inside my heart.

38.

THE BUS ON THE CLIFF

THE COUNTRYSIDE OF Southern India is mesmerizing. Everything feels so exotic. Today we're headed out on a nature excursion into the wilderness. The road leading up to the nature trail we're going to turns out to be exceptionally narrow. It is, in fact, so narrow that branches of the trees on the left side of the road are pressing against our bus and pushing it to the right. This would have been fine if there were a sidewalk or some bushes on the right. But oh no! On the right side of the bus is a cliff. A very steep cliff, with a drop of hundreds of feet beyond it.

Down below us is a river with a strong current. Winding tornado-like shapes are making their presence known all over the water. Suddenly a big branch shoots straight into the bus through an open window! It is a miracle that the girl sitting next to the window doesn't get hurt.

The bus has now stopped. We can't go any further. The bus is too large for this small road. Indian men are running past the bus, squeezing by it to get behind us. Then, to my absolute fear, we start backing up.

I'm in my own dream! The dream I had earlier in the retreat. This is the same bus, and there is the same cliff. In the dream, we fall down the cliff, but we're all safe.

I immediately know this is a test. That's, of course, why I had the dream prior to this trip. I'm faced with a test to see if I can fully experience where I am, and fully trust I'm safe even in extreme uncertainty, no matter what happens. With my eyes on the road behind us, I feel love all over my body and visualize the bus backing down the hill safely.

Whether it is divine intervention, sheer luck, or my powerful visualization and inner trust, it works. I pass the test! After a few minutes of watching Indian men running and screaming, and pushing the bus, our driver is able to reverse it down the narrow road and we make it back to safer ground. I'm in awe by this exercise in ultimate trust. More than anything I feel gratitude.

The bus driver takes us down another road to a serene location with lots of trees, wild grass, and open spaces. We've come here to connect with nature, and I walk around the grounds admiring the setting.

I've always loved nature, but I don't think I've ever felt this connected before. I touch a tree with my left hand and just hold it for a long time. I'm able to take in all that the tree is experiencing, everything: rain, wind, and sunset. Then I place my right hand on the tree and send it love and grace, and pray to feel separate from my mind's activity.

As I stand up, a big mountain catches my gaze. I know this is a sacred place. My feet feel like they have suction cups underneath them, firmly rooting me to the ground. I sit down on a small rock, my heart fully open, and for the first time in my life I can really feel the stillness, like I actually belong here. I wish I could stay here. It's such a beautiful experience. I am floating out in all directions and I am one with everything around me.

39.

"ANGER IS NOT YOU"

DURING DINNER LAST night, Enrique and I exchanged a long, exciting look. As I was coming back to the dormitory, I found a little chair on the grass. I sat there looking up at the stars, thinking the heavenly lights in the night is the world's best kept secret. I hoped Enrique would come and join me, and he must have felt the energy as well, because he showed up just a few minutes later and sat down next to me. He told me about his life back home, and how he lives in a small, rural village in northern Spain surrounded by mountains.

He loves being alone, he said, and easily gets hot. When I told him I was always cold, he laughed and asked, "Why do I always meet girls who get cold?"

We talked some more about the process here at the retreat. I told him about the nature excursion and the bus incident. Curious to hear more about it, he asked me, "Did you feel much anger during the experience?"

"No," I said, a bit surprised. "Just a lot of worry, fear, and sadness."

"Ah," he says, "anger is not you."

This seemed strange to me, as I had actually felt a lot of anger in my life. I guessed he meant that anger was not a domi-nant part of my personality, whereas fear and worry probably were. That must be why I have experienced those feelings here more than anger while working on myself.

We sat there for a long time, gazing at the stars. The energy between us was electric, even though all he really did was sit close to me. It just felt magical to be so close to him. Then they came, the words I did not want to hear. "You know," he said, "I met a girl here in India last year. She lives in the States. It's difficult doing this long-distance thing."

"Oh," I said, trying to sound cheerful and understanding at the same time. "One of you has to move." I was trying to be supportive, although this was not at all what I wanted him to do.

"Yes," he said, "but it's very difficult."

"You must be very much in love," I suggested.

We smiled and sat in silence for a while. Before we said goodbye for the evening, he came close to me and said, "We should talk some more." It was seductive. He made me tremble just standing near me.

I went to sleep praying to meet Enrique in my dreams. As the angels would have it, he did show up in one of my dreams. This dream was a lot shorter than my dream with Brahman. All there was was a kiss. It was the most magical kiss out of this world! I woke up feeling refreshed, but somehow knowing this was the end of our little love saga.

40.

DIVINE INITIATION

IN INDIA, THE transfer of divine energy from a guru to a disciple is referred to as *initiation*. This is a sacred process that accelerates a disciple's path to enlightenment. Enlightenment may not happen instantaneously, it can take many years, but once initiated, the disciple's awakening process has begun. Today was a special day. We received our initiation!

The initiation began with a sacred ceremony held this morning in a white building near the ancient temple. As I walked through the doors, I was met by music, the miraculous sounds of St. Francis prayer in a song. The words "Lord, make me an instrument of peace" filled the entire room with divinity and grace. I felt so blessed and honored to be there. I prayed for my heart to open and for divine love to flow through me.

Each of our individual dasas personally initiated us by placing their hands on our heads and transferring Brahman's energy to us. It was when Nicolita lovingly placed her hands on my head to give me the initiation that it happened. Everything went light. But the light was not coming from outside me; rather my whole head was being lit up from within, from a space deep inside my skull, behind my eyes. My head was filled with light! I think what I was experiencing was kundalini rising!

Kundalini is an immensely powerful energy force that lies dormant at the base of the spine. It can be released when we're in high spiritual states, and once activated, it travels up the spine like lightning and cascades out through the top of the head.

I must have been in a pure state of consciousness, because all of a sudden I saw an enormous orb above one of the dasas. It was bigger than a soccer ball and shining like a radiant sun. *Everything is glimmering today,* I thought.

After the initiation, we danced around the room. I was in such a wonderful state of love and joy. We received malas to wear around our necks. These are white wooden-bead necklaces used in both the Hindu and Buddhist traditions to stay focused when meditating. I felt so filled with love dancing around the room wearing my mala.

After returning to the ashram, we gathered in the meditation hall. Everyone was still full of joy I think – after a while people began laughing loudly. But this time around I didn't wonder if they were actors because I was now one of them! I lay on the floor laughing uncontrollably for a period that felt like an eternity. What I was experiencing was sheer joy.

Eventually, the laughing eased and there was only happiness everywhere. I looked around the hall and took in the light atmosphere. People looked so alive.

As I studied my surroundings, I noticed a girl at the front of the room. I hadn't had any contact with her to speak of throughout the retreat, but then again, I hadn't really had any contact with anyone here! A few times before I'd found myself wondering if she might be an angel. She had the most gorgeous, radiant light blue eyes and there was an adorably warm energy about her. The girl must have noticed me looking at her because she walked over to me with a loving smile on her face and said, "I think you're an angel!"

I looked at her in surprise, eyeing her radiant face. "That's funny," I said, exclaiming, "I think *you* are an angel! I've been walking around thinking that all along," I add brightly.

We both laughed.

"It takes one to see one," she chimed in.

I was mesmerized by the coincidence. *Isn't it funny how you can be seeing something in someone that the other person is seeing in you!*

I learned that Annie lives in San Francisco. About half an hour later, I ran into her again at the Indian restrooms behind the meditation hall. I call them *Indian restrooms,* as they are equipped with simple holes in the floor and have no western-style toilet seats. Annie looked at me and gave a little giggle. "Oh yeah, most definitely you are!"

Just as I was walking back into the meditation hall, Ananda suddenly appeared in front of me. She is the French woman from room four whom I felt so intriguingly allured by in the beginning of the retreat. We hadn't spoken at length since the very first day at the retreat when the other women in our room were clucking at her like a brood of hens in disapproval of her nudity. I smiled at Ananda and gave her a hug. I was curious to find out more about her. We began talking and she told me she lives in southern France, where she helps couples through romantic art therapy.

Aha! There we had it. This is, of course, why I felt such charged energy when I was around her. She was a sensual goddess inside and out, and her career was an amazing fit for her. Funnily enough, this time I didn't feel the same fascination for her that I did earlier. Even so, I was happy talking with her.

As I sat down near the front of the meditation hall, I saw a girl with long blond hair headed in my direction, glancing uncertainly at me. "May I tell you something?" she asked, whispering so quietly that I could hardly hear her. I had seen her every day throughout my stay here. She had never seemed very confident and I could tell she was hesitating. She almost seemed scared to talk to me, but at the same time there was also an eagerness to share whatever it was.

"Of course," I replied, gesturing for her to sit down next to me, giving her a reassuring smile.

With tears in her eyes, she took a deep breath. "OK, so this is a little strange . . .," she began, then stopped and cleared her throat. "It's just that you've played such a big part in my personal process here. I don't know if you have noticed me looking at you, but I was. There is something about you. I see the person in you that I've always wished I could be."

"Wow," I said. I paused and looked her straight in the eyes. "If you see it in me, then you have it in you!" I smiled at her. That was probably the nicest, most special thing anyone ever told me.

We enjoyed each other's company for a while.

41.

KEEP A VISION

NAMASTE IS THE essence of how I want to live my life from now on. I want to perceive and honor the Divine in everyone and everything, including myself, and to feel connected and grateful. It's our last day at the ashram and the buses that will take us to the airport are already waiting outside the dormitory. What an incredible soul journey this has been. I feel so much love and gratitude.

I hug everyone. It's been less than a month, but we have shared a journey of struggles and beauty. The retreat was a magical time of blissful silence, going within, healing emotional patterns, releasing stories, surrendering to pain, and connecting with divine energy and eternal love. Now it's time for all of us to go in our different directions. A few of the girls are heading up north, planning to travel around India for a while. I'm going back home, and my plan is to spread love all around the world.

My first stop will be my company's London office!

At the airport it feels fun to see so many people mingling about. I make my way to the first-class lounge, where I enjoy a plate of delicious nuts and fruits. Everything tastes good and I feel absolutely wonderful. I must be radiating happiness from top to toe. A lovely elderly couple sits down opposite me and the lady gives me a warm smile. Ah, how the world feels good right now! I reach for my journal, and decide to write down whatever observations come to mind. I love contemplating ideas and perspectives, and I am very grateful that I spent so much of my time in India writing in my journal. I've had so many beautiful insights and now I can go back and read them whenever I need a little reminder. Although most of the teachings from the dasas have not been new to me intellectually, what's been different this time around is that I was able to actually actively live these principles. Before I came here I thought I knew so much, but the truth is I wasn't dedicated to my spiritual path on a daily basis. *That is why the retreat has been so exciting,* I think. *I really hope I'll be able to continue living in this higher frequency from now on.*

At the beginning of the retreat, when I sat down and spoke to Nicolita about my life and career, she told me something very important. "Don't live a moment without having a vision in your life for yourself, your family, your success, your career, and the world. Having a vision is how you will come to feel fulfillment and contentment." This could very well be one of the most important lessons I am bringing home from my time in India. It probably supersedes many of the other truths and lessons I'm coming away with. After all, intention is one of the most powerful energies in the universe. *Without knowing what we want, how can we get it?*

I believe staying focused is what gives us purpose. *Working toward something is for sure more exciting and rewarding than simply walking around in a confused daze.*

I close my eyes and think about my mornings here in India. Every morning felt sacred. I loved how we began every day with a peaceful meditation in which we reminded ourselves to accept our personalities and looked to see if there was something difficult on our minds.

There is simply no running away from the tiger. We can never have freedom *from* something, only *with* whatever is going on. The best way to handle fear or anything we are struggling with is to stay with it, not run away. The process of simply observing that we are trying to escape helps us to "jump into the tiger's mouth."

In my journal I write:

> *By becoming more aware of ourselves, it's easier to notice if there's a part of us that needs more love, understanding, and acceptance. Whenever that is the case, and it often is, of course, it's important that we nourish this particular part in all kinds of ways. Otherwise, this aspect could slowly transform into external situations that will keep on showing us what we need to see and learn. Until we do address such parts, life can be a very painful process.*

This is good, a wealth of brilliant insights are coming forward just from jotting down my thoughts on the paper.

During the retreat, the dasas would often remind us that our thoughts are not our own. One of the male dasas put this concept very nicely into words the other day when he said, "We are not saying you cannot think. Thoughts are very useful, when used correctly, and when they come out of your heart. What we are telling you is to develop a practice where you begin to observe your thoughts and notice how they come and go."

What I have come to see through nonstop meditation over the last few weeks is how thoughts definitely come and go. It's tempting to follow them, but there really is no need to put our attention on every single thought that comes our way. With time, if we just let them be there, they move further below us and we gain a bird's eye view of them, which makes it easier for us not to feel affected by them.

Ideally, thinking should be used only to help solve the problems we want or need to solve, or to ascertain the steps we need to take to achieve our visions. Right now, I'm thinking about everything I wish to remember from my time in India, and how I best can make use of everything I've learned. Now isn't that an excellent way of engaging in thought!

42.

GOLDEN INSIGHTS

RETURNING HOME FROM somewhere exotic, or after a long trip, is always a peculiar experience. I can't help wondering what it will feel like this time. The dasas reminded us several times yesterday that we could expect big changes to occur when we return home. They urged us to pray for help, no matter what happens, whether we're experiencing a conflict or an emotional discharge.

Ah, all those emotional conflicts. I wish they could disappear forever. I remember one of the dasas once saying something so beautiful. "Just be yourself. This way you will experience less conflict!" If that is the answer, I sure hope I can always be myself.

Regardless of how many tools I have, I would rather not have to deal with conflicts anymore. I'd love to get to a place where I don't need any tools because I have no conflicts.

When I told Nicolita that one day, she laughed and said, "Conflicts come to show you that there's a dissonance some-where. They help bring awareness to a situation. With time, you'll experience less conflict." Then she added, "Always re-member, while you're working hard on trying to change your life, what you really should be doing is focusing on what you are projecting. The life you are living is playing out on a movie screen. It shows you what is happening inside of you. The world you see is a reflection of your inner condition, of where you are right now.

"You don't need to change other people. Work on yourself. Once you change within, your life will automatically improve."

I am so happy that I met Nicolita. She has a way of putting everything so eloquently into words. I have no doubt that I will remember what she said when I get home.

I sit back and look around the airport lounge. Travelers are mingling and the ambience feels exciting. *Isn't it strange that I would have to come all the way here to see that I've been looking at the wrong image? All this time, for my entire life, really, I've been focused on how other people are behaving, when the person I should have been putting my attention on was me.* Right now everything probably feels inspiring because I feel so good and I have cleared so many blockages. I am the one who is creating the experiences I have.

No wonder I've always been fascinated by holograms. Because a hologram is created by images of the same thing taken at different times and angles, the resulting picture contains areas of interference. There are a lot of images everywhere in my life made from an original source: me. I'm the source of what I'm seeing. If there are patterns of interference, they depend on when and how I projected the images into the hologram of my life.

◆◆◆

One thing that I am really bringing with me from our daily meditation sessions is the power of prayer. I lovingly learned firsthand how something we pray for with all our heart can happen that instant, such as when Brahman looked at me the very second I made my wish. This was also what happened when the fairy appeared in my room the same night I prayed for something miraculous to happen to me.

Why do some prayers work so quickly, whereas others take time? I bet the dasas would say it depends on our beliefs. "Do you really believe in what you pray for? Do you really believe it will happen?" they would ask.

If we are clear about what we want, really want it and believe we will have it, and we have a relationship with the Divine in our hearts, our prayers become powerful. Then it's a matter of surrendering and feeling gratitude that the prayer is blessed and fulfilled. If we don't believe in what we want, staying with the helplessness we feel is how room opens up for the Divine to come in and help.

Last week, before one of our meditations, one of the male dasas—a man who in my eyes looks a bit like an Indian version of Matt Damon, and is really quite cute—explained something I've often wondered about. When asked, "What about the prayers that don't come true?" his answer was, "If you don't see your prayer coming through, the problem may have been fixed another way, or possibly the prayer helped change something within you so that whatever issue you prayed about no longer disturbs you."

I very much believe this last idea is true! By reaching a new state of awareness, an issue we first had problems with is no longer an issue. A new solution may have come along, or we may not even see something as a "problem" anymore, but now a blessing.

One thing I know. My time in India has been a divine blessing. *The biggest journey of my life and isn't it funny how I spent most of the time traveling within myself?*

PART II

43.

"TONE DOWN THE LOVE BUSINESS"

"A DECAF COFFEE, please, and a plate of fresh fruit," I say brightly to the waitress at the Marriott Hotel in London. "Oh, and may I please have the coffee in a to-go cup?"

"Certainly, Miss Bjorklund. It is such a pleasure to have you back with us," she responds in her elegant English accent.

I am excited to be back in the "outer world." If anyone who shared the sacred time with me in India were to see me right now I doubt they would even recognize me! I'm dolled up with makeup, my hair is smooth and shiny again, and I'm dressed in one of my immaculate off-white suits, wearing high heels, and back glitzing around in beautiful hotels.

I happily sip on my coffee as I grab a taxi off Gloucester Road to the office. Traveling through London invigorates me from head to toe. There is so much life. *Almost like India, but different*, I think. I smile as I gaze out the window. I'm back in a world that focuses more on the outer than the inner, but the world doesn't feel sad or vain. It feels fun and refreshing. *Life is about being balanced,* I remind myself. *We need to live both inside and outside.* It's important to eat healthy, and it's also okay to have a little treat here and there. We need our beauty sleep, and it's okay to stay up late every now and then. Meditating and going within helps us in miraculous ways, and we also have parts of us that love connecting with others and expressing ourselves.

Everything feels good. I'm on top of the world. I'm walking around in something of a love bubble. I've been back at our offices in London for a week now and I'm greeting everyone with love, literally. I'm not only hugging people left and right, but also placing my hands in Namaste pose whenever I feel grateful, which is pretty much all the time.

The other day, one of the directors of the company called me into his office. He gave me an amused little grin, then said, "AK, I'm so happy for you that you are able to share and spread so much love, and I actually think this is all really cool. I do." His face suddenly turned serious. "But today when meeting with the our new investor, just tone it down a bit, OK? Tone down the love business."

I nodded politely, but as I walked out of his office, I couldn't help laughing. I must look like a shining star walking around smiling, high on love. That is just how I feel right now. I vibrate on a frequency of love. No doubt I will feel sad and angry again, uncertain and worried again; but when I do, it will be temporary. I just need to experience each feeling until it passes. I have the tools down. It's sure going to be fun going back to the United States tomorrow. I'm ready for the rest of my life to begin.

44.

WAVES OF LOVE

WHEN WE APPROACH Los Angeles, it feels like I'm flying in with a whole new perspective on life. My serenity must still be radiating all around me, because just as we are about to prepare for landing, an elderly gentleman in an elegant charcoal jacket approaches me. He flashes me a white smile and gestures at my hands, which are folded in my lap. "I can't help noticing how peaceful you look. May I ask, have you just been to a spiritual retreat or something?"

"Yes, I have," I say and beam at him in surprised excitement. "I just returned about a week ago." He gives me a knowing look and walks back to his seat. I smile to myself. I am so very peaceful right now.

Heading home to Laguna Beach, driving along the scenic coastal highway feels so inspiring. This is my home now. I've lived in many places over the years, but California occupies a very special place in my heart. As the driver pulls into the driveway of my little seaside cottage, the first thing I see is what used to be my black Mercedes. It's now so covered in dust that it almost looks white. That's OK. I am happy to be home. I can get out a hose later and rinse it off or go to a car wash. I tip the driver and walk into the house. I don't think I will ever forget this moment. The energy is serene. There is love in the air.

Suddenly it dawns on me, *I will never again feel alone.* I stand in the middle of the room and gaze out over the sea.

I pick up the phone and dial Richard. It takes less than a ring for him to pick up. He must have been waiting for me to call! "Hi! I'm back," I say, smiling with my whole heart and face. "How was it?" he asks. His deep voice comes through the line and I can't help feeling a little jolt of excitement. "Did you get to that space in-between your thoughts? I bet you're very skinny!"

Richard and I chat for a while. After hanging up I think, *Hmm, I'm not exactly skinny. I wonder what Richard will say when he actually sees me. I probably have put on several pounds from loving everything I eat so much these days.* The idea of weight gain no longer bothers me however, I just love life! We're having dinner tonight, so he'll get to see for himself then. It's funny. Normally I would be freaking out over some extra pounds, but now I just feel content.

I unpack my things, carefully taking out the photos of Brahman I purchased in India. *I'm going to get some pretty frames for the photos. Especially this one.* I hold up a photo of Brahman wearing a golden kurta, a type of hip-length collarless cotton shirt that many men in India wear. When I look into his eyes I know this is not just a regular picture. *The dasas were right. The picture* does *carry energy.*

I find the CD I bought before going to India of V chanting Brahman's mantra. Sitting down on my big, round rug in the middle of the room, I close my eyes and listen to the angelic tones of her chanting voice. I played this music every day before my trip and I haven't heard it since I left. It feels so wonderful to be hearing her voice again, and the familiar mantra. Suddenly I hear footsteps coming up the stairs of my little cottage. *Oh my. Oh my. This is it. I'm going to see Richard again, after all this time. I can't wait to share my trip with him.* I open the door and all I feel is love. Love flowing in all directions. I can only imagine what my eyes look like, because they feel like glistening diamonds. We embrace and I'm in heaven.

We end up walking down the street for dinner at a little Thai restaurant around the corner, and I tell him how peaceful everything feels. "Since I got back, it's sometimes hard to think, I don't even want to. I just want to be still, inside," I share.

"That's how I feel all the time," he shrugs his shoulders. I recall that he's a long-time meditator. He continues, "You know, it's the space between the thoughts that is everything, right? That's what real silence is all about."

I knew there was something special about Richard. He gets it. He is very evolved. I don't know much about him as a human, and what personalities he struggles with, but I know his soul is beautiful.

45.

TWINKLING STARS

I'VE BEEN HOME for a few weeks now, and I'm still experiencing so much joy wherever I go. My love for Richard is flowing in all directions as well. Thank goodness the only observation he made about my new, slightly rounder shape when I returned was, "You feel different." The first night back in California, I fell asleep in his arms and the most amazing thing happened. His energy felt like Brahman's! It was like Brahman was there, or that he was Brahman. I was embraced in a field of infinite, divine love, and fell asleep wishing with all my heart and soul to one day have a child with this man.

Richard and I celebrated Valentine's Day together yesterday. We enjoyed a romantic dinner at an elegant restaurant that was so fancy they didn't even have menus or prices. The waiters suggested courses, but you could order pretty much anything you wanted. We had lobster, salmon, desserts, the whole shebang. Even though I usually love drinking red wine with dinner, I didn't have any. I feel so pure right now and I don't dare jinx it by mixing in wine.

The best part of the evening was walking around the art shops in Laguna Beach. I was enthralled by the art. I think I gazed at one painting for as long as ten minutes. The love was flowing out of my heart. It was like I was one with the painting, and all I could see was beauty.

One odd thing I've noticed lately is how dogs seem to feel the elevated energy around me. Their reaction is rather peculiar. This morning on the beach a few dogs totally lost control and started jumping for joy when they saw me. A similar situation happened this afternoon with two other dogs going totally berserk when I walked by them, going wild with happiness. I never quite had this effect on dogs before.

Something is in the air. It's got to be all the Indian love energy. Whatever it is, I love it, and it makes me share it with people around me, which I love even more.

Something wakes me in the middle of the night. As I open my eyes, the first thing I see is a field of twinkling little lights—they could be stars—together forming the shape of a bell and flying over my stomach. I open my eyes wide. All I feel is love. Everywhere. Once the "lights" notice that I am conscious of them, the whole field somehow goes straight up and just disappears.

I've had a few visions in my life, including a vision of a golden orb filled with millions of geometrical shapes, the little fairy who appeared to me right here in this room a few months ago, and visions of quite a few spirits, but this is something new. There was so much light! The field of lights was shining as if from infinity, and felt immensely loving and intelligent.

If it had been the early morning hours, I would probably had gotten up right away, but it is still the middle of the night and there is not much else to do but go back to sleep, so I do. I know I have just witnessed a real miracle. There was nothing ordinary about these lights. Someone, somewhere is communicating with me.

46.

A Wish Is Granted

As I drive up along Pacific Ocean on my way to work this morning, I can't help thinking of the twinkling "stars" that illuminated my room last night. *Who is trying to send me a message?* As I pull into the parking lot at my office, it suddenly hits me like a bright flash of intelligence. *Could I really be . . .?*

I make a quick stop by my desk to check for any urgent messages, and luckily there is nothing that has to be sorted out this very minute, so I run back to the car and head over to the local CVS drug store. I swiftly find my way down to the women's health section, where I grab two pregnancy tests.

The girl at the counter smiles at me and says, "Yay or nay, right?"

"Yes, right." I smile confidently back at her. I already know the answer. *The Universe is saying yes.*

I'm now waiting in the ladies' restroom, holding a pregnancy test stick in my hand, and sure enough, it has a clear plus sign on it, broadcasting pregnancy on every possible frequency. I wrap the stick carefully in tissue, place it in my bag, and go back to the office.

My manager sits at the desk across from mine. As I sit down, I flash him a wide grin. I'd better not tell anyone just yet, not even him.

My goodness, how early can it be? A few weeks? Is this why I've been shining so much, and why dogs have been acting so bizarrely around me? Can dogs smell pregnancy?

I pick up the phone and dial Richard. He's on his way to Los Angeles and won't be back until Sunday, he tells me. Oh dear. Now I have to wait. I can't tell him something like this over the phone. It's only Thursday. The wait is going to be so long.

I meet with my friend Kristina in the evening and tell her that something extraordinary has happened to me, but I can't say yet what it is. Oh, I so wish I could!

◆◆◆

Richard finally gets back on Sunday and comes over to my house. I already told him I have something important to tell him and I can tell he is nervous. He is trying his best, however, to look relaxed. I sit down on the sofa opposite him, and with big eyes and an open heart, I tell him my news. "I'm pregnant. I mean, I think I am. I'm pretty sure I am. I've taken a few home tests already, and they all say I am. Actually I know I am."

His answer is short and sweet, "Oh boy!" is all he says, which pretty much paints the picture. He's quite surprised.

As he leaves the next day, I can't help thinking about how strange the situation is. How could I have become pregnant in the first place? My body must have been so balanced from meditating all day long in India that the flow of love energy running through me has made me blossom into a vibrant flower. Then I remember. *My wish.* The night I got back, I made a deep wish to one day have a child with Richard. *Oh heavenly miracles. My wish must have been granted instantly because I was in a place of infinite flowing love.*

My wish came true sooner than I would have ever imagined, so now a divine baby is growing inside me. I wonder what this means to Richard though? He's a lot older than me, over twenty years my elder, and he may even feel he's ready to retire. It probably wasn't the best thing to do when I suggested we watch *Father of the Bride 2* with Steve Martin the other night, which happens to be one of my favorite funny movies. In fact, he told me it gave him stress and he looked rather overwhelmed when he left.

Richard may simply be too old to be doing the fatherhood thing all over again. He already has kids from when he was younger and married. With or without him though, this is the most miraculous thing that has ever happened to me, and I feel inspired by it. This must have been why those twinkling stars appeared over my stomach the other night! The baby's soul was coming into my body and communicating with me through these lights.

47.

A STAR IS BORN

THE MONTHS ARE flying by. Richard and I have moved to a beautiful home, and I've been decorating the baby's nursery with so much love. Richard's ex-wife, Lolita, has turned into a wonderful friend of mine, and she even hosted my baby shower a few weeks ago. It's funny. I'm interestingly not feeling uncomfortable over his old relationship with her—not at all. Our new friendship makes me think of how much jealousy I used to suffer from before going to India. One thing is for sure, although I may not have cleared every emotional pattern and personality quirk while I was away, I'm certainly not as jealous as I used to be. Lolita put on a very pretty baby shower at her beautiful home, and my mom came all the way from Sweden to be there as well, so it was a very precious time.

Since the shower, the baby's drawers have been bursting with precious little pink clothes. We already know we're expecting a girl. Richard could not join me at the ultrasound session, so I had the nurse write the gender down for both of us on a piece of paper, which she carefully sealed inside a small yellow envelope. Later when Richard and I opened the envelope together I could tell he was genuinely happy. The note read: *"She's a girl!"*

I was over the moon with excitement. I've always wished for a little girl.

It's now only a week to go before my due date. I have a large pink bag packed with clothes for me and the baby for when it's time. The bag is standing next to the door in the baby's room, and every time I walk past it I feel a little jolt of excitement.

I'm actually going to the hospital today for a "stress test." It sounds so funny. This is my third time doing this. The baby isn't putting on much weight and I'm extremely thirsty all the time. In the first "stress test," my baby's heartbeat went down when she was exposed to a high-frequency sound, rather than beating faster, which is the standard response to stress. Afterward, I was given another ultrasound, and the doctor discovered that I had hardly any amniotic fluid left. So now I come back every second day for another test to ensure everything is going well with the baby.

"Lay down here and place these stickers on your belly," the nurse tells me with a warm, caring voice.

I look at the screen beside me. It shows a moving picture of my baby's heart rate. Sure enough, the same thing that happened earlier occurs again. When they try to put my daughter under stress, her heart rate slows down instead of rising faster. I smile to myself. Little do they know that this is a miraculous baby conceived in total bliss and love. I've been meditating every day throughout my pregnancy, so it's probably going to be hard to scare her!

The nurse walks out the door. I follow her with my eyes and see her consulting with a doctor in the hallway. I can't help feeling slightly nervous. *Could something be wrong?* I do my best to experience the situation fully, as I was taught to do by the dasas at the ashram, but before I get a chance to truly feel anything, the nurse returns.

"Do you have your bag packed?" She asks, smiling joyfully at me.

"*Erm* . . . absolutely . . . but it's at home!" I reply, looking up at her expectantly from where I'm lying.

"Well, then, you'd better have someone bring it over, because you're not leaving this hospital. We're taking you right up to delivery!"

I laugh to myself. I'm probably one of very few mothers-to-be who drove themselves to the hospital to deliver a baby the same day.

◆◆◆

My daughter is born a few hours later. I bet all mothers say this - she is the cutest baby I've ever seen. As she looks at me with her big, round, bright eyes I am embraced in eternal love, and I feel home. Her name is Angelina.

48.

GROWING DISSONANCE

I LOVE MY baby more than anything in the world. In the midst of all joy though, my life is far from smooth sailing in paradise. I was doing so well in India inside the protected walls of the ashram. Now back in California, it's quite clear that I haven't mastered the spiritual lessons I was taught yet.

My relationship with Richard has become rather tense lately. I love his soul, but he's not an easy man to live with. He gets very worked up emotionally, and seems to be angry all the time these days. At the end of the day, I honestly think he would be better suited for an adventurous life in the tropics.

Some days I get a glimmering spark of higher awareness and realize I may in fact have created the outer conflicts I'm experiencing in order to help me learn more about myself and my "different personalities." Other times, I live in a confused daze, blaming my discomfort on the outer world.

My biggest challenge however is not my relationship with Richard. I haven't told anyone this yet, because I feel scared even thinking the thought myself. It began a few months ago while I was still pregnant. One day, I noticed an uncomfortable sensation in my body when I was participating in a friend's event honoring Brahman. It suddenly became so intense that I had to go and lay down. My heart was beating double speed and I was shaking for minutes. Then, a week later, right after my beach class, the physical reaction occurred again, leaving me outright exhausted, nauseous, and sweaty. Some days the racing of my heart would become so intense that I couldn't do anything else but to lay down and rest for hours after coming home from an event.

At first I persuaded myself that I was shaking because the energy was too much for the baby. But even after giving birth, I am now still experiencing the same type of physical reaction. Leading sacred meditation groups in Brahman's name has played such a big part in my life since returning home from India, so I'm not sure what's going on. I remember the dasas telling us that if we ever have a strong reaction to the energy it's because it is activating something within us that we need to work through. It's a purifying energy; whatever is activated must come out.

What if the resistance I'm experiencing is a wake-up sign of some sort? What if it means that this is no longer the right path for me? I've been trying to give in to whatever has been stirred up inside me and just surrender, as I was taught to do in India, but it's a frightening sensation.

Most of all, I'm scared of hurting Brahman with my thoughts. After all, we're sharing the same divine energy. It's now part of who I am. I am his devotee. *Oh no. I don't dare thinking about it anymore. I had better keep this to myself. I won't say a word to anyone about my doubts. Hopefully everything will turn out OK, and I will feel wonderful again soon.*

49.

WHAT HAPPENED TO MY PATH?

LAST WEEK SOMETHING peculiar happened. On some level, I may have pulled this event into my energy field because of the growing inner dissonance I've been experiencing lately. Or it may just have been a coincidence. To be fair, I don't really believe in "coincidences," so I'm assuming that one way or the other, what happened occurred for a reason.

I had just finished feeding Angelina on the sofa when one of my meditation students phoned. She was crying hysterically and it was difficult to understand what she was saying. Between sobs, she told me, "I met two girls from France the other day. When I told them about your Saturday morning meditations and how you've been to an ashram in India, they said they had also been to an Indian ashram and how they suffered a mental breakdown when they got back home because the guru took away their power. I'm so afraid that this Indian energy experience could be hurting us. Is that possible?"

I sat down and let her vent, While listening intently to her, I gave her all my love, and reassuringly said, "Ah, Louisa, I can definitely understand how some people would find the experience of staying at an ashram overwhelming, but our personal power can never be taken away from us."

"But why would they have such a hard time after coming home?" she asked.

"I'm not sure, but I do know that working on ourselves is an extremely tough process, no matter where we are. In fact, I remember seeing some people at the ashram having a very hard time," I said. Then I paused before thoughtfully adding, "All I know is that it's always important to trust our intuition and stay with whatever we're feeling. You obviously met the girls right now for a reason, and we don't know why. There may be something within you that needed to hear their remarks at this particular moment in time."

I must admit, it was a bit of a shock to receive this type of phone call. I thought, *What if there is something within me that needed to hear this information as well?* Then I remembered the heavy effect the process of fully experiencing sadness had on some people at the ashram: Some were screaming and shouting hysterically. There is no doubt that this energy can be power-ful. It facilitates pure divine connection and activates all kinds of healing processes, which obviously can be a struggle while you're in the midst of it. It sure is interesting, though, that my student would call me right when I'm beginning to wonder if it may be time for me to move on. Is there any truth to this? *Am I losing my spiritual connection?*

I spent less than a month in India, but it felt like years. Every day I was looking and feeling within, in total silence, healing and integrating my personalities. My whole existence there was so different from my daily life at home—and from anywhere else I've ever been for that matter. The process was tough, there's no question about it. It was definitely not a dance on rose petals. But spending my days and nights in total stillness and silence, contemplating on my pain or just meditating without any outer interference, was sure a lot easier than handling all day-to-day events at home. I came back with so many beautiful teachings, but I'm obviously not living them, or I would not feel like this. *There is more work to be done here!*

I pick up the phone and call a woman I know who visited the same ashram a few years before me. After I tell her about the conversation I just had with my student, she gently says, "These types of reactions are so common." She pauses to reflect, and thoughtfully continues, "You know, working on ourselves can be challenging, no doubt about it. It can be even harder once we come back home and are no longer protected by a serene environment and support system. What is important for you right now is to listen to your heart and feel what is real. Both of us have felt the tremendous love that Brahman has for us."

We talk further about the trials and tribulations some people experience, and how intense an inward process really can be, especially for someone who has a lot of unprocessed pain. In those cases, an inner journey on a silent retreat could simply be too much.

For me though, I don't really feel that the real underlying issue with the dissonance I'm experiencing is unprocessed pain. Rather I get the sense it has more to do with the aspect of devoting myself to someone else's life path rather than honoring myself. I want to create my own destiny and reach my own insights, rather than embracing someone else's wisdom. *No matter how much love I feel for Brahman, perhaps it is not part of my soul path to be a devotee anymore.*

My thoughts turn back to Richard. *Oh. It's so hard experiencing him right now. I'm actually beginning to feel the time may even have come for me and Angelina to move into our own home.* It is interesting to me that I would consider leaving both Brahman and Richard at the same time. There is clearly something big occurring inside me and I am trying to escape it. I already know it. *You can't run away from a tiger. I just don't know how to stop.*

50.

TWO BREAKUPS

THE OTHER DAY I was walking with Angelina in the stroller when we suddenly passed an angel card reading shop. I had passed it many times before, I just hadn't paid attention to it. This time I stopped. With all my heart I knew that I had to go in. My heart was crying out for clarity. Maybe an angel reading would shed some light on the situation.

An elderly lady with curly white hair came to the door and lovingly welcomed us inside. The front of the building had beautiful displays of vibrant crystals and incense. She led me into a small room in the back with a square table and two chairs. As she laid out a spread of cards, she praised me for being a spiritual teacher, but then she stopped and said she saw something troubling me. She remained silent for a while, and then asked, "Do you feel like you're always trying to please someone else? Or like there's not much room in your own life for you?"

In her question was my answer. It made perfect sense. After all, that was exactly how I've been feeling lately. Since Brahman came into my life, my life has become all about following in his footsteps and honoring his energy. There is no room for my own spiritual path anymore. That could very well be why I attracted the phone call from my meditation student, Louisa, to help accelerate whatever process of soul growth I'm now in.

I went back to the angel store this morning and asked the old lady if she might be able to help me clear my energy field a bit. I sat down on a white sofa in the front of the store while she checked with one of the energy healers who works there. After a while, a woman named Mary came out of the back room. As soon as I saw her I knew this meeting was divinely called for. She looked like a saint. Mary and I made plans for me to come and see her on a weekly basis until I feel myself bouncing back again.

I had my first session with Mary this afternoon and it felt great. For the first time in a long time, I feel as if I am honoring myself again and my own soul path. All of a sudden it becomes clear. I am afraid of losing my freedom, and for that reason, I need to say goodbye to Brahman. My soul is yearning to blossom into its own potential, and not walk in someone else's footsteps anymore.

Last week, after visiting the angel reading shop, I finally decided it is time for me to leave Richard as well. I'm feeling more focused and independent now. Bizarrely enough, just like praying in Brahman's honor felt like I was living Brahman's life rather than my own, living with Richard actually felt like I was honoring him more than myself.

No matter how much Richard and I love each other, we have different dreams. It's better we just have a loving and happy family when we choose to be together, but the rest of the time it will be better for Angelina and me to live on our own in our own home. I just know it.

Everything is going to be OK. I have my job and I'm a self-sufficient and free woman.

51.

ONE DOOR CLOSES

"**WHAT?**" **I RAISE** my voice, unable to maintain my calm and feeling a slight sensation of panic coming over me. "Complications? Issues? What exactly are we talking about here?" I take a deep breath, trying not to sound too anxious. "What is going on? This just can't be right!"

My attorney responds in an apologetic, but firm voice. "I'm so sorry Anna, let's set up a conference call with the London office, OK? There are a few options that could work for you, but we're going to have to figure out a solution pretty fast or you could find yourself on a plane back to Sweden before you know it."

I put down the receiver and sit still for a while. I can't believe what I just heard. I've been in the United States for a long time now on renewable business visas. My company began a green card application process for me earlier in the year, and we all thought that the approval process was coming along fine. I am in utter shock because my attorney just told me that we have to wait eight years before even being able to be considered for a green card. The category we filed under has apparently been inundated by applicants.

On top of it all, I've now had my maximum quota of two business visas, and also received an extension, which was granted to me because of all my overseas travels. I'm not even allowed to apply for a new business visa. The application has to be for a green card, and time is running out. My current visa expires in just a few weeks. *Oh my goodness!*

I take a deep, conscious breath. It's pretty urgent that I open my eyes and see what's really happening. For some reason, the Universe is guiding me in a new direction, and whether I want to or not, there is no other way to face it but jumping right into the tiger's gap.

I think about Nicolita, and what she would say. She'd probably advise me to stay with everything. I definitely need to observe and accept where I am, not just wrestle with it. *Maybe this is an exercise in trust, to help me see that I can find happiness in any situation, no matter what life throws at me?*

52.

UNSAFE WATERS

IT'S A PRETTY easy observation: I'm in unsafe waters and I feel cornered. This morning I had a conference call with the attorney and a representative from the London office, who pretty much told me I have only three options. I can:

1. Go back to London
2. Become a full-time student
3. Get married as soon as possible

Options One and Three are both out of the question at this point. I can't leave the country. Angelina is an American citizen and Richard would not be happy with her moving overseas. At the end of the day, I wouldn't want to take Angelina away from her dad under any avoidable circumstances. No matter how much hardship we've been through, I love him deeply and I want Angelina to have a good relationship with her father. On top of everything, this is where we live. This is our home.

I also can't get married. How could I possibly find a new man to love in the next two weeks? Although I still have Richard in my heart, marrying him would make me feel like I've lost my freedom. I don't fully understand why, but I'm scared of feeling like I'm living his life rather than my own.

I'm looking at Option Two. As I wonder, *Could I?* My heart takes a little leap with joy. I have always dreamed of studying dreams and psychology, of finding ways to understand life's bigger questions. Suddenly it dawns on me that the door to get a green card through working for my company may be closing for a reason. This could be a big blessing. Who knows what will come out of this? This could be my opportunity to do something that resonates more with me, something I've always dreamed of doing. Perhaps this is helping me follow my soul's true life path.

Angelina and I now live in an adorable little community right on the waterfront in Newport Beach, the same area I also lived in when I first came to the United States years ago. The familiarity feels good. Our place is small and quaint, and the energy is divine. It already feels like home. We have a picturesque walking bridge to a small island, where I walk almost every day. Every morning we wake up to the sounds of seagulls and barking sea lions, and then breathe in fresh ocean air all day long. In the night we fall asleep to the soothing sounds of the ocean. The lifestyle fills me with so much inspiration. I can't give this up. I don't want to.

This is where we live. This is our life.

It's not a hard decision to make, the signs are all pointing me in one direction. I'm going to become a full-time student.

This is becoming a spiritual exercise in trust. Again I think of Nicolita and what she would say, probably something along these lines: "When you accept anything as a beautiful state in itself, you can experience everything and be happy!"

This situation may be an initiation test. If I can find happiness in uncertainty and hardship, I will evolve. It's all about having the right perspective and attitude.

53.

ANOTHER DOOR OPENS

A FEW DAYS after the phone call with my attorney, I run into my friend Nancy. When she tells me she's doing a master's program in counseling psychology at a nearby university, my mouth drops open of excitement. *This is exactly what I want to do!*

I look up the school the next day, and apply there and then. The campus is close to home so I won't have to spend most of my days commuting, leaving Angelina with babysitters for hours on end. I was totally meant to meet Nancy.

The admission interview with the dean goes well. It turns out that we share the same passionate interest in depth psychology and Carl Jung, which makes me feel even better about attending this school. Through a miracle, I am accepted on the spot and become a graduate student in counseling psychology!

Studying dream psychology has been something I have wished to do all my life. Now that it's finally happening I can't quite believe it's taken me this long to get around to doing it. I send out farewell messages to my colleagues and clients. Not everyone in my life shares my enthusiasm, however. Whereas some of my colleagues and clients have been understanding and supportive when I told them the news, others are outright shocked when they hear about my new field of study. One client emailed me four question marks. It's interesting how some people react in a similar confused way this time around, similar to when I went to India. I guess some clients still view me as a corporate girl who just wants to be jetsetting around the world. But of course I have many personalities. I love the good life and adore staying in luxurious hotels and leading business meetings, but there is an equally big part of me that yearns for something bigger and deeper. I yearn for meaning. I want to understand more about everything. I want to find the answers to life's big questions.

Many people are genuinely happy for me though and it's wonderful to get their well wishes. Some of my clients have even shared their own dreams of starting over fresh and embarking on a new and more soul-fulfilling career. An aircraft planner for a major airline told me he dreams of writing children's books. A hedge fund manager told me that he dreams of owning a coffee shop. Another client told me she dreams of opening a yoga studio and doing yoga every day. We all have dreams, and I'm going to make mine come true.

I had my first class this evening and it was quite a rush! This is going to be good for me. I'm doing something for my soul again! The feeling I have is similar to the feeling I had when I left for India. The journey I began in India is now continuing because I'm back on my path, only this time it's my own soul path and not someone else's.

54.

"SOMETIMES A DRAGONFLY LANDS ON MY FACE"

IT WOULDN'T BE true to say it wasn't challenging at times to raise a daughter while being in graduate school with very limited funds, but somehow we miraculously kept making it work every month! I've graduated now, and I can happily say I enjoyed every day of my studies. If there was one passionate student on campus, it was definitely me.

I've been reading books by Carl Jung for many years, but it wasn't until this time of my life that I truly fell in love with all of his amazing teachings and insights. What an incredible soul. Whereas most of my colleagues seem more drawn to branches of cognitive behavioral therapy, I doubtlessly resonate more with Jungian depth psychology.

It's kind of interesting how it's all unfolded. Most of my professors didn't share my interest in Jungian psychology at all, and some of them even shared with me how they initially would have preferred that I concentrated on a subject area they felt more familiar with themselves, but my passion and enthusiasm seemed to have rubbed off, and I was actually able to focus on Jung in the majority of my courses. My path as a Jungian graduate student did not happen by chance, and I am so grateful for all the help and support I received. I'm even holding workshops in depth psychology for doctorate students!

◆◆◆

I'm now putting all my studies into practice, working closely with therapy clients as an intern at various locations, including a children's clinic. One of my first clients here was an eight-year-old boy who was sent to me for the treatment of depression. As we began meeting more regularly, I soon understood that there was another scene playing out behind the curtains. I doubted he really was depressed, but something was evidently troubling him.

A few weeks into treatment he began feeling more comfortable talking with me. He then shared a secret that had been buried deep inside him for a long time. I don't think I will ever forget this moment. He suddenly blurted:

"Sometimes a dragonfly lands on my face."

Upon hearing his words, I sat straight up in my chair and looked at him with curiosity. "A dragonfly?" I asked in an interested tone.

"Yea, actually there's a lot of them, and they have different colors. They are in my dreams, too. Sometimes they are in my room, mainly at night . . . but in the daytime, too," he said, and then added, "I just saw one here in the office."

I turned around and looked behind me. I didn't see any dragonflies. *This was so fascinating! What were the chances of receiving such an interesting case so early in my career?* I thought. I knew I had to be careful when presenting this case to my supervisor. If I didn't emphasize how there could indeed be an imaginary component, he may possibly be sent out from the center for further evaluation, and risk end up getting diagnosed with some kind of bizarre hallucinations.

The "dragonflies" the boy described seeing were not visible to anybody but him. He told me how he sometimes could feel them physically, as if they were resting on his face. Other times they just flew around the room.

I was naturally very eager to get to the bottom of all this. In my weekly meeting with the clinical director, I mentioned the case, but chose not to go into great detail. I simply shared that I was working with a boy with a vivid imagination. I felt it was important to keep working with him myself for a few more weeks before discussing this further.

As therapy progressed, my intuition told me that the right thing to do was to make the boy feel more comfortable with his little friends. By encouraging him to introduce them to me, and allowing him to talk about them freely and to draw pictures of them, it soon became evident that they comprised a multitude of different feelings. Their shapes and colors changed depending on what "they were feeling" or . . . and here comes the punch . . . *depending on what he was feeling!*

It soon became clear that not only did the dragonflies have feelings of their own, but that they also represented feelings that had not yet been fully developed in the boy. I spent a lot of my time pondering on the boy and his guests. It was all so fascinating to me. Then I remembered reading something Jung once said. In one of his books, he discussed how unconscious repressed content can split off from the conscious mind as an independent complex and live a separate life in the unconscious.[1] If I hadn't come across this, I don't know if I would have ever considered that the boy's dragonflies may actually be complexes within him – that now were living lives of their own – literally!

This boy truly intrigued me. I took him through a range of imaginary exercises, including art therapy and dream work, and throughout all exercises, I had him carefully identifying his feelings. What happens next is the most astonishing thing. He slowly began reintegrating his feelings back into his body. As his awareness of his feelings increased, the dragonflies were no longer showing up as frequently. One day they were completely gone!

It's now been a few "dragonfly-free" months. The boy is still coming to the center for check-ups, but I must say, it's looking very promising. Just the other day he told me he hasn't seen one in a long time. How his situation has resolved fills me with so much awe and inspiration. This is a boy who used to be troubled by these visitors on a daily basis.

When I finally shared the entire case with my director, she told me she was very pleased with the results, and even remarked, "Isn't it interesting how you would get this case, Anna? You keep getting the most extraordinary cases I've ever heard of in my entire career."

I smiled knowingly. *When the student is ready, the teacher appears,* I thought to myself. I was ready to help this boy because of my studies in Jungian psychology. I'm sure a higher power had something to do with it, perhaps helping me to connect with this boy somehow from somewhere outside of time and space.

This incredible case has really helped me see the immense power of our inner worlds, and reinforced my understanding of how an internal situation or dissonance can manifest in what we think of as the outer world.

55.

INTO THE WEB

I USED TO think I would come back from India as a new woman who had mastered all her emotions, but even now with a graduate degree in psychology, I recognize that is clearly not the case. At a party yesterday when the host asked me to introduce myself, I got nervous again! That old familiar feeling of anxiety flowed in like a thick wave, clenched my chest, and took over my entire body like I was attacked by an alien. Thankfully it soon went away, and I know I'm doing a lot better than I used to, but I really feel it's no longer just enough to have the tools. I want the anxiety gone.

What's more . . . my love life is still unhealthy as well! I keep attracting men who make me feel like I've lost my freedom. Whatever it was that I was trying to avoid when I stepped away from Brahman and Richard is obviously not healed - especially when it comes to relationships. I wonder if there's a deep underlying pattern that is behind all of these similar life situations?

A while ago an old friend of mine came back into my life and we soon began dating. He was flowing with financial abundance, and I must say it was really nice having some of the pressure lifted off my shoulders, after all the struggles I went through making ends meet as a single mother throughout graduate school. He truly stepped into my life as a knight in shiny armor.

I felt so happy in the beginning of our relationship, but it wasn't long until it turned into a somewhat uncomfortable situation. Once more, my old relationship patterns of being too devoted and pleasing too much began playing out. This time around though, there was more to it, because I had now also become dependent on him financially, and I felt controlled. My sense of freedom was yet again in jeopardy, and I felt like I was honoring someone else's life path over my own - again. We broke up some time ago now, and Angelina and I moved to a smaller place, but I'm still suffering. More than anything, I'm disappointed in myself for attracting situations where I soon enough end up feeling excluded from my own life, like I'm being pushed off my path. The time has come to untangle this web once and for all. Like the dasas said in India – what happens in my life is a reflection of what's going on inside me!

Angelina is at school and the house is quiet and peaceful, so I decide to lie down for a bit and reflect on my life. *Maybe the answer will come to me if I go into a deep sleep with the intention of bringing any destructive patterns out in the open.* I open up my dream journal and place a bookmark where my last dream ended. I always keep it on top of the nightstand, so I can easily find it when I wake up. My dreams have helped me so much over the years, especially when it comes to knowing and accepting myself on a higher level. Best of all, they keep filling me with so much faith and inspiration – emphasizing how important it is to make wishes, like this one:

> *I am at a café and notice how I can stretch out my iPhone to an iPad and back! I show my friend, and I am so excited because I have been wishing for an iPad. I tell her I wished to find money and I did (earlier in the dream), and how I wished to have an iPad and now I do. I am so excited and amazed my wishes are coming true.*

I've had dreams where I changed the color of the sky from blue to pink, met with an old wise man, created food out of air, found money, met the President, was loved and praised by spiritual leaders, and even recreated life situations altogether.

Amazingly, in many of my dreams there is an angelic woman there somewhere in the background, and sometimes she's walking next to me teaching me something. I can't help wondering if she could be my higher self – perhaps visiting me in this consciousness from a more advanced level of awareness. I once asked her, but she just smiled at me. Whoever she is, I know she cares about me immensely, and she is always near.

I close my eyes and drift into a serene state of deep meditation. Suddenly I find myself back in India. I am walking through a pretty Indian garden, decorated with vibrant orchids and a large statue of Ganesha. I observe how extraordinary it is that I'm having this wondrous experience somewhere inside myself, somewhere in time, somewhere in space. Or perhaps a better term would be somewhere *outside of* time and space?

It's been a couple of years now since I started dreaming about time. Time travel, time as a concept, time as a means of changing things around us and undoing or recreating past situations. If there really is no such thing as time, as some philosophers and scientists have posited, then everything we experience occurs at once, including different lifetimes. Maybe it's possible to heal ourselves on every level at any point in eternity. Over the last few years, I have often asked my dreams for guidance about what steps to take, but to be honest I have seldom asked to understand myself on a higher level.

What if I'm caught in a timeless emotional pattern that I will be entangled in for eternity unless I heal from it? This is the paradox I'm facing. If there is no such thing as time and everything really happens at once, it is crucial that I heal whatever it is I'm facing. If I heal in one place, I heal everywhere. I feel myself floating out into a vast field of illuminated golden energy. I pray with all my heart and soul for eternal clarity: I want to see all of my personalities. I'm ready to listen to myself on a deeper soul level and disentangle the emotional patterns I'm trapped in.

56.

THE GIRL AND THE DRAGON

AS IT TURNS out, I don't need to wait long for insight. Like a magnificent painting, a dream from some years ago reappears and unfolds in front of my eyes. I still remember it like yesterday. Now that I think of it, I had this dream right around the time I cut my energetic ties with Brahman. I named it "The Girl and the Dragon."

> A beautiful Native American girl with long black hair is riding alongside a river on a horse. She is moving in the upstream direction. The time period is about two hundred years ago. Down the river comes a modern yacht carrying a group of young, rich and successful bankers laughing and enjoying themselves. The "old world" on the bank of the river meets the "new world" on the boat.
>
> Suddenly an enormous, dark black dragon appears from the riverbed. His whole body rises up in front of the young bankers' yacht. The dragon sees the beautiful girl. The dragon grabs the girl in his fist and holds her very tightly. The bankers are afraid that the dragon will kill the girl, and they feel guilty. The dragon, however, warms up from the beauty and kindness of the girl and he does not hurt her. He just holds her tightly. The girl knows she needs to sacrifice her freedom to stay alive.

This is definitely what Jungians would describe as a *big dream*. It is filled with archetypal elements like fairytales and legends. I'm so astounded it would come back to me right now.

I get up from the couch, walk into the kitchen, and pour myself a glass of lemonade that I squeezed earlier this morning. I gaze out the window, looking at the beautiful boats in the harbor. I love clear days like this one. I wish I could feel as clear about the true meaning of my big dream and how it relates to my life.

It's intriguing, to say the least, that I would remember the dragon dream today. As I recall, when I first had the dream, it left me with mixed feelings. There was an insight that kindness would conquer evil, but also sadness. The Native American girl's life may have been saved by her beauty and kindness, but now her freedom is lost. *Hmm. I wonder. Have I lost my power to the dragon?* Maybe this was what my client Louisa was referring to a few years ago –when she called and told me about the girls who felt they had lost their "power" to the guru.

Perhaps most fascinating of all to me, looking at the dream in hindsight, is how it took place in different zones. The Native American girl from the past was moving forward through time on the river when she encountered the modern-day bankers and the timeless dragon. Coincidentally, dragons are symbols for time in China. Doesn't that show something playing out on a deeper level! What an amazing soul gift - my own unconscious has borrowed the archetypal image of the dragon from the collective unconscious to symbolize the energy I need to work through on a timeless level.

In the west, dragons are often portrayed in myths as guardians of treasure. *If this were for me, could the dragon be trying to protect, guard, or control a personality perhaps? Or could it be a sign that one of my shadow personalities is behaving like a dragon?*

I can see how all the characters could play a role within me. The indigenous girl could stand for my spiritual and motherly devoted self, but also the helpless part of me that so often feels controlled, whereas the bankers could represent my masculine power, and the part of me that feels guilty for having put myself in this position in the first place.

I wonder if the dragon could symbolize feelings that I have repressed - such as my sense of power, self-worth, or my anxiety? Or maybe my anger? I'm definitely not at ease with any of these.

Now that I think of it, I've experienced a lot of anxiety throughout my life, especially when it comes to talking about myself. Since anxiety is often a mask for something that we fear unconsciously - *I wonder what I'm afraid of?*

I've traveled around so much in my life, which has been fantastic, but it may have been too much. Sometimes I don't even know where my home is, or where I belong. In fact, I don't think I even know who I really am. I may be afraid of not belonging anywhere, not feeling accepted, and not feeling good enough.

That may also be the reason why I have put up with so many unhealthy relationships along the way. I keep seeking connection, acceptance, and a sense of belonging outside of myself, and I end up devoting myself too much to people around me, and giving up my power in the process.

No wonder the dragon is so enormous. I am not honoring myself and my own power is projected on people around me, and that's of course why I feel controlled and anxious! I am overpowered and controlled by my shadow, stuck in an emotional pattern - I have attracted an archetype of devotion into my life.

Of course I can't run away from the dragon, he represents my shadow, fed by an emotional pattern within me – of not feeling connected within myself. There is no wonder I have attracted similar situations over and over.

One thing I know, it's only through love and higher consciousness that the girl in my dream will ever get a chance to see that she is connected to the dragon – and that this powerful force is part of her whether she likes it or not. The lack of freedom that I have continued experiencing all these years will not be healed until I learn to live from my heart, love all aspects of myself, and call back my power. Likewise, I can't push away my anxiety, as I am the one creating it. There can be no separation between the personalities. Running away from the dragon won't solve anything, because all the characters are *one*. All my life I've been running away from myself. There is no wonder I don't know where I belong. I haven't felt worthy of loving myself.

My heart takes a little jolt of excitement, and suddenly I feel a bright light of divine insight illuminating my entire being, and this is when it occurs to me: *I am conscious of my pattern, which means I am healing!*

57.

SELF-LOVE

IN MANY WAYS, I know it was the process of becoming so totally devoted to Brahman that ultimately helped bringing my deep underlying emotional pattern to the surface, but I wasn't yet ready to see what was happening at the time.

I know what I need to do. It is time to find my own connection, embrace myself with love, accept and appreciate all parts of myself, including my repressed feelings, and step into my own power. If I at the same time could also welcome Brahman back into my heart and find a way to honor him and my own spiritual path, I think that would be the ultimate soul healing. That seems to have been my problem over the years – loving myself and someone else at the same time.

Determined, I quickly walk down to the garage and locate my memory box. It's neatly stored on the top shelf with some old CDs and other treasured items I've acquired over the years. I bring it back into the house and place it on the kitchen table. I am practically trembling with excitement. I haven't looked inside this box for so long. *Oh, I so pray it's still in here. My first-ever Indian mantra CD, chanted by the Norwegian woman, V, whom I met right before going to India.* As I take off the lid, to my astonishment, there it is! A CD with a beautiful white cover embellished with golden text is lying on top of all the other memorabilia.

Distancing myself from Brahman was an intense emotional experience for me. I was so terribly conflicted. I felt so much love for him, and there was a deep layer of guilt in my heart for leaving him. Even hearing the mantra chanted back then felt overwhelming, and I eventually ended up putting away all my Indian CDs.

The justification I gave myself at the time for ending my devotion to Brahman was my fear of endangering my own spiritual freedom and path. In some way, it was almost like I felt controlled by the organization. I so wished to belong to his dasas and become his devotee, but instead I ended up feeling like I lost my independence.

All the pieces are flying together at the speed of light. What I was lacking was self-worth and self-understanding, and because I wasn't living in reverence with my soul, there is no wonder I felt disconnected from my spiritual path. But this had nothing to do with Brahman. Now that I think of it, I was on an eternal quest for more freedom long before going to India. Who knows how long I have been ensnarled in this pattern!

The bliss of experiencing the golden energy fields and the magnetism of different spiritual experiences were part of the allure that took me to India. But underneath my desire for these experiences was a hidden longing for something greater. My soul was yearning to feel worthy, connected, loved, and free.

58.

TALE OF DEVOTION

WITH A FLASH of insight, it suddenly dawns on me how there are parallels between me and the boy who saw imaginary dragonflies everywhere he looked. He had problems recognizing his feelings, so they consequently became separated from him. They split off and took on lives of their own. He projected his feelings on colorful imaginary dragonflies in order to help him see them. It was only by lovingly accepting his feelings outside him in this form that he was able to gradually reintegrate them back into his body.

My own repressed fear of not being loved and accepted began living its own life as a split-off power projected on situations and people around me in order to help me see what was happening to me internally, which in turn made me feel anxious and controlled. It's pretty clear why I attracted this little boy into my practice. I may not have had bugs all around me, but our situations and major energy patterns resembled each other in a particular way. There's even a good chance we share the same healing path. *I helped the boy accept all his parts. Hopefully I have what it takes to do the same for me.*

When the boy was able to talk about the bugs and accept them, not only were they integrated with his feelings again, but best of all, they were no longer needed. He stopped seeing them.

The moment I can find a way to lovingly appreciate who I am and call back my power, hopefully my pattern can be healed too. *Oh, how Carl Jung would have loved this story!*

Love is flowing all around me. I finally see it. All those years ago, when I suddenly felt uncomfortable and wanted to run away from Brahman, I didn't have the consciousness to understand what was happening. At the time I thought the only way to feel "empowered" again and escape the discomfort I was experiencing was to completely go my own way, but my plan backfired. Soon enough I ended up in new situations where I felt even less free than before.

At the time it didn't occur to me to work through the sensation of powerlessness within myself and take responsibility for the dissonant feeling I was experiencing. I assumed it was outside me and being done *to* me. I assumed I was the victim and only had a choice to leave or to stay and play a passive and subordinate role.

The dasas in India used to remind us to believe that our prayers can come true. Nicolita would say something like, "If you don't believe in yourself, how can you accept yourself?" Beyond the supposed power struggle with the dominating figure of whatever the dragon du jour might be, the deeper underlying issue I've always been experiencing is my ambiguous sense of identity. Because I've always been so uncomfortable with my anxiety, and often felt overpowered by my own emotional reactions, it has been hard for me to love, trust, accept, and honor different aspects of my identity, which seems to have been a breeding ground for my poor boundaries in relationships.

Of course, more than anything, I need to learn to love and revere all parts of myself. By hopelessly devoting myself to someone else in a heartfelt attempt to belong, and putting all my eggs in someone else's basket, mentally speaking, I've only been putting more fuel in the fire, trusting myself less instead of accepting and loving myself for who I am.

59.

A Blossoming Heart

In India, the dasas always reminded us to invite grace into our lives whenever something gets hard or we don't know the answer. I take a deep breath and pray to God to be able to love, accept, and honor myself. It is by believing in myself that I will be able to find wholeness in my heart, and live in reverence with my soul instead of always trying to look outside of myself hoping to belong somewhere else.

I close my eyes and think about a dream I had last night. The teacher in the dream, who likely represented my own inner spiritual teacher, was trying to point out how loved and appreciated I am, and how much value I bring to both others and myself:

> *I meet, embrace, talk with, and kiss one of the most powerful male spiritual teachers I have ever met. It is a very loving encounter filled with happiness, but most of all, I feel the teacher's appreciation and immense gratitude for what I do, and the value I bring to this world.*

Isn't it interesting how this dream unfolded last night? All day I've felt embraced by love. The time has come to handle any dilemma that comes my way with trust and gratitude, and this dream came to remind me that love and connection I'm longing for begins within.

I won't find true love anywhere else, no matter how much I seek, or how far I travel, unless I'm first whole inside. I've entered a crucible of soul healing, and the way to the golden connection I've been seeking for so long is not to run away from inner struggles, but to let the alchemical healing process unfold by staying right where I am.

I hold the mantra CD with steady hands and close my eyes. I imagine Brahman in front of me, smiling to see where I am right now. This is going to be a beautiful part of my healing process, I know it. I am going to go into my own heart first, and then connect with Brahman.

I insert the CD into the computer drive, copy the music into a song list, and then let its magical sound fill the room. I sit with my legs crossed and spine straight, and breathe in deeply. As if a sliding door has just opened, I feel myself back in India again. There is so much peace. I am seated in the meditation room, dressed all in white, bowing to Brahman. There are flowers everywhere—so much beauty. I drift back and forth between now and then, here and there.

I feel Brahman smiling at me again, and suddenly sense a pair of hands on my head. There is no physical person in my room, but I know that he is here and giving me his love. I send my love back to Brahman. I am sharing my love like a sun, with an open heart; the light is pouring out of my chest. The love is ever flowing. I sit for a long time, healing in the immersion of my own love.

After my meditation, I walk into my closet and pick out a white cotton shirt and a white pair of jeans. I want to be dressed in pure white today, white from top to toe. I put on a necklace that is strung with the tiny Ganesha figurine I wore in India. I slide into a white pair of wedges and grab a white handbag off the shelf. Being dressed in white is the vision I used to hold of myself while I was in India, which brings a smile to my face. I used to joke that one day I would be known as the girl in white with a bindi on her forehead. *I can skip the bindi,* I think, laughing to myself, *and I don't need to wear white every day. But today is special.*

My heart is like a blossoming lotus flower. Wide open. The day has come for healing my soul in eternity. From now on I pledge to love, accept, and honor all parts of myself, flourish into my full potential, and live from my heart. I intend to lead my life from a state of love.

60.

A Few Years Later

"**THAT WAS SO** much fun, mom!" Angelina beams brightly at me.

Angelina just turned seven a couple months ago, and she looks like a little angel with her wild blonde hair and green sparkly eyes. She's wearing a long white dress with a red silk ribbon around her waist and has a green-leaved Lucia crown with little white candles on her head. I'm in the same picturesque attire myself. We're in the Holiday Show at our town's theatre, bringing Sweden to the stage, performing as Santa Lucia - which is a Swedish light celebration that takes place this time of the year. We started doing shows together just a couple years ago. I bend down and give her a big hug. Suddenly she gives out a little shriek of joy and runs over to her side of the counter in our dressing room, where someone has placed a big round plate filled with Swedish lussekatter. Lussekatter look a bit like cinnamon buns, but they are made with saffron instead of the cinnamon. With her mouth full, she turns to me and says,

"We are a team mom!"

"Yes we are!" I say, smiling at her.

I love being on stage, not only does it give a wonderful avenue for expressing ourselves fully, but it also helps bring more awareness of all our parts, as well as aspects of others. It's all about enhancing our consciousness and awareness, I think to myself as I pack up our bags. The show tonight was the first time I performed solo on stage, and even though I felt nervous, it was an entrancing experience, and the anxiety did not control me. It may be baby steps, but I'm for sure heading in the right direction, expressing myself more and more and living my life more fully each day.

It suddenly occurs to me how my main wishes in India - to work with dreams, write books, sing, and be a mother, have all come true! Over the last few years I've appeared on TV shows talking about dreams, written a book, singing more and more, and given birth to my daughter. I am creating my life!

The moment I decided to become comfortable with my anxiety, appreciate myself for where I am right now in my level of consciousness, and above all, live with gratitude in my heart, was the moment my emotional well-being blossomed. I began accepting my anxiety as a feeling that occurs whenever there is a part of me that feels fearful of being judged and rejected, and now see it as a sign that I need to go back into my heart, and give myself some more love and appreciation.

The healing effects from walking the path of self-love has had positive reverberations in my relationships as well. The interesting thing is the moment my inner energy began shifting, I no longer feel pushed off from my path. I feel aligned with my own heart and connected with myself. Today, I no longer feel like I'm at risk of losing my freedom, or that I'm living my partner's life in a relationship. I have found my inner connection, and I am finally able to be devoted to someone else and myself at the same time.

I am also more connected to people around me. The focus is no longer on whether or not people like me, but instead there is a lighter energy of joy and appreciation unfolding, and it is coming from my heart. With gratitude, love, and compassion, everything becomes a lot more fun, and it feels a lot better too!

61.

A GOLDEN JOURNEY

THE ANCIENT ALCHEMISTS believed it is first necessary to work on our inner states before anything can be transformed on the outside[1]. My trip to India was the beginning of what I think of as a major alchemical soul transformation. Meditating from morning to night and breathing in the divine spiritual teachings of the dasas was like entering an immense crucible where emotional breakdowns helped dissolve old emotional energy. It was a blissful experience that healed me on several levels emotionally and prepared me for the somewhat rocky road that followed.

In fairytales, the hero conquers big battles on his grand journey before finding the pot of shiny gold. On a soul journey, the ultimate mastery comes from learning to love and accept ourselves for who we are, reaching higher awareness of our personalities, and lovingly honoring our souls in everything we do. Becoming aware of our personalities and underlying emotional patterns is not an overnight phenomenon however. It took me many years of dedicated dream work until I was able to understand the emotional pattern I had been ensnarled in for so long. Gaining higher awareness of ourselves is an ever-evolving process, and to live in reverence with our soul and lovingly accept all of ourselves, are the sacred components that fuel the alchemical transformation of our divine soul growth.

In the process of writing my story, I decided to reach out directly to the ashram in India to share my story of inner healing and soul transformation, and I also took the opportunity to thank Brahman for helping me love and understand myself on a deeper level. One of Brahman's dasas wrote me a kind letter back, and he also gave me a list of people that I might enjoy connecting with here in the United States. One of them was a man who lives in Los Angeles, which is only about an hour away from me. I met him for coffee one day, and his eyes twinkled as he said to me, "Brahman is not a guru in the sense you may have thought – he does not want people to follow him. His golden calling is to inspire seekers to find their own divine." I smiled when I heard this, because I knew it was true.

Brahman has a sacred space in my heart, and I see him as a master who helps me connect with the Divine, so I am very grateful with all my heart that we reconnected. But something has shifted in our relationship. Today, I hold many masters in my heart, and I know that we can have more than one spiritual teacher. When we open up our hearts and allow ourselves to be loved, an abundance of sacred teachers, divine beings, and dream guides appear by our side. All we need to do is to stay open and live in trust. Best of all, I have found that the most sacred teacher of them all is my higher self. The connection I traveled so far to experience was found within me.

The timeless journey I embarked on represents all of us, and the dreamy trials symbolize the alchemical process of healing and lovingly transforming into something higher and brighter. Deep down we all share the quest to live our life to the fullest, and let our souls blossom. By reaching higher awareness, honoring our soul growth, living everyday with loving intent, inspiration, passion, and gratitude, we flow in love and freedom and transcend time.

I think I'll always be a searcher, on an eternal quest for higher awareness. It is by no means necessary to travel across the globe to embark on a spiritual adventure though. A soul journey is an inner experience that can unfold anywhere. Living in reverence for our soul, warmly accepting and loving ourselves with compassion, living from our heart, and connecting with others from a place of love, is the golden key to soul transformation.

The gold we are seeking is found within.

Namaste.

Anna-Karin

NOTES

Preface
Epigraph.
1. G. Lachman. *Jung the Mystic: The Esoteric Dimensions of Carl Jung's Life and Teachings* (New York, N.Y.: The Penguin Group). 2010. p.157.
2. M.L. Von Franz. *Alchemical Active Imagination.* (Boston, MA.: Penguin Random House). 1997. p.37.

Chapter 33. A Dreamy Life
1. Carl G. Jung. *Dreams* (Princeton, N.J.: Princeton University Press). 1974. p.78.

Chapter 54. "Sometimes I feel like there's a bug on my face"
1. Carl G. Jung. *Collected Works of C.G. Jung, Volume 16: The Practice of Psychotherapy,* edited by Gerhard Adler and R.F.C. Hull (Princeton, N.J.: Princeton University Press). 1966. p.56.

Chapter 61. A Golden Journey
1. M.L. Von Franz. *Alchemical Active Imagination* (Boston, MA: Penguin Random House). 1997. p.40.

ABOUT THE AUTHOR

ANNA-KARIN BJORKLUND is a dream expert and writer. Her first book was *Dream Guidance: Interpret Your Dreams and Create the Life You Desire!* She holds a bachelor's degree from the University of Technology in Sydney, Australia, and a master's degree in counseling psychology from Argosy University in Orange, California. Originally from Sweden, she is a passionate traveler and explorer, and has lived in five countries.

www.AnnaKarinBjorklund.com

Made in the USA
San Bernardino, CA
29 March 2019